"Razor-sharp wit with an unusual flair for the grotesque."
—*Montreal Gazette*

Jan Lars Jensen was the Everyman novelist, a quiet Canadian librarian who struck gold when he sold his first novel—a dystopian tale set in a future India—to an American publisher. Soon, though, he began feeling as if something was coming unhinged in his mind, and true madness enveloped him as he was revising the book for his editor.

After attempting suicide, Jensen woke in a psych ward bed, with the ideas that had once inspired him now roaming through his mind as waking nightmares. But just as literature had prompted his disastrous slide, so did it help him rebuild and recover. Whether struggling to comprehend James Herriot's animal tales through a haze of anti-psychotic medication; deciphering his psychiatrist's references to Patrick O'Brian's novels; or attempting to steer himself toward sleep with a history of logging, books defined Jensen's world.

Nervous System chronicles Jensen's unique experience, from his conviction that a nuclear apocalypse would be provoked by his novel, to his fragile recovery, and belated discovery that a course of the anti-malarial drug Lariam for an aborted trip to India may have contributed to his breakdown. Gripping and unsettling, darkly humorous and deeply moving, *Nervous System* is a tale of literary madness like no other.

"Exhibits intelligence, wit and charm. The Jan of the memoir is a gentle and perceptive soul, under attack by his own nervous system and incredible imagination." —*Victoria Times-Colonist*

JAN LARS JENSEN lives in Calgary, Alberta, with his wife, Michelle. His first novel, *Shiva 3000*, was published in 2000. His short fiction has appeared in *Descant*, *Prairie Fire*, *Geist*, and other periodicals around the world.

Nervous System

or,

Losing My Mind in Literature

Jan Lars Jensen

CARROLL & GRAF PUBLISHERS
NEW YORK

NERVOUS SYSTEM
Or, Losing My Mind in Literature

Carroll & Graf Publishers
An Imprint of Avalon Publishing Group Inc.
245 West 17th Street
11th Floor
New York, NY 10011

AVALON
publishing group incorporated

Copyright © 2004 by Jan Lars Jensen

First Carroll & Graf edition 2005

First published in Canada by Raincoast Books

Library of Congress Cataloging-in-Publication Data is available.

ISBN: 0-7867-1562-6

9 8 7 6 5 4 3 2 1

Printed in the United States of America
Distributed by Publishers Group West

*This book is dedicated to my wife Michelle,
and to Michael Kandel,
two people who rose above.*

*Some names and identifying characteristics have been changed.
Some dialogue has been reconstructed from hazy periods,
and should be viewed as fictional. The order of some events,
while I was delusional, may be incorrect.
There may be factual mistakes. If an episode seems overly
dramatic or poorly described or if my word choice seems off,
I was probably on heavy medication.
Read with caution.*

PART ONE

The Singing Marksman

NIGHT TWO

LYING IN BED, I waited for my killer.

I fully expected him at some point during the night, but I was disturbed by how he chose to make his presence known.

"She'll be coming round the mountain, when she comes ..."

He sang.

He stood outside, unseen, and I listened to him singing the same lines over and over.

"She'll be coming round the mountain, when she comes ..."

The song seemed a perverse choice, from him. A cruel joke. Perhaps he'd been drinking, in preparation for this moment. Maybe he needed to be drunk to do his work. Or ... he didn't know which room was mine. Yes, that was it. He wanted me to go to the window. This was his way of getting me to show my face so he would know where to shoot, or which room to break into. He wanted me to look at him out there, crooning.

"She'll be coming round the mountain ..."

I waited. My throat felt very dry.

The singing stopped.

What did that mean? Had he gotten inside?

A terrible thought occurred to me. What if he chose the wrong room? What if he came inside to get me, but mistakenly killed someone else? People are hard to tell apart, under sheets. What if he killed several innocent people in his effort to find me?

I got out of bed and left the room. The hallway was empty. I checked in both directions, then walked purposefully, briskly, toward the brightly lit cube with the big windows at the end. Inside sat a woman in white, and I moved to the front so I could speak, quickly, through the scooped slot where glass met ledge.

"There's someone outside who's going to come in here," I reported. "He's going to try to kill me."

The nurse looked at me. "How do you know someone outside wants to kill you?"

"I heard him," I said. "Singing."

"Dude!" Another patient stood nearby, a skinny guy with a crest of puffy blond hair. "Dude, no, that was me. I was in the smokers' room, singing."

The smokers' room was next to mine. "Sure," I said.

"Dude, I promise you, it was me you heard!"

I turned back to the nurse. "I want to stay out here, so when he comes he'll have a clear shot."

The nurse exhaled. "Fine."

The skinny guy watched me walk to the midpoint of the hallway and sit, leaning against the wall.

For the safety of the other patients and staff, this was the best place for me to be. I could be seen from a distance, and from whichever end of the hallway my killer appeared, he could fire a headshot with little chance of the bullet passing through a wall into another room. I sat and waited. This was the best I could do.

A patient emerged from her room and shuffled to the nurses' station. Going by, she didn't look at me. Her slippers never left the floor as she walked — *slowly*. Hurry up! Get out of here! What if the assassin came now? At the nurses' station, the woman said, "— keeps blowing and blowing and won't turn off and—" I willed her to leave. I looked from side to side as she talked. Eventually, she was ushered back to her room, still talking. A nurse walked toward the emergency exit.

"Please don't go near that door!" I shouted.

The nurse came down the hall toward me. "I was only checking that the ward is secure. And it is. The ward is secure."

"I would appreciate it if you don't go close to the doors."

"You've been sitting out here for almost two hours," she said. "Nobody has come. Nobody is coming. Will you please give us a break and go back to your room?"

Reluctantly I stood and did as requested.

My room was small. A room of this size, with limited furnishings, provided few options. Except for the floor.

I lay down on the tiled surface with my feet below the window and light from outside illuminating my face. This way, when the marksman came to the window, he could plainly see it was me, and have the easiest possible shot.

ADMISSIONS

THAT WAS MY SECOND NIGHT in the hospital. I had arrived the evening before, thinking, *Well, I finally get to find out what it feels like to have my stomach pumped.*

Being someone who gags easily, I had always dreaded such a moment. In my youth I'd heard the process described — a tube stuck down your throat, a machine pumping and whirring at the other end, the contents of your stomach filling a laboratory container, probably in plain view — and I had taken care never to swallow a key or a box of matches or anything else that might necessitate the procedure. But tonight was different. This was the most different night of my life, in the life of everybody, of the entire world, the most significant period in history, the end of humanity, basically, and I would take whatever discomfort or pain or humiliation might be coming. That was fair. Because I was to blame.

My co-worker's husband Klaus had driven me from the library to the hospital. Though we had never been more than casual acquaintances, he gave me a brief hug before turning me over to the admitting nurse in Emergency. I admitted: I had taken twenty or so sleeping pills. My wife Michelle was crying. *How did she get here so quickly?* I hadn't seen her arrive, and her presence surprised me. I wasn't sure what to make of her tears, either. I was quickly shuttled over to a doctor, to whom I explained my actions as best I could. He seemed busy but gave his full attention.

And he must have known more about the prescription that I had abused than I did, because he didn't call for a stomach pump, only a wheelchair. I did feel woozy.

Most of the hospital, the Emergency room and the corridors branching from it, the places I knew from breaking my ankle and visiting sick relatives, followed a colour scheme of teal and pink, which I associated with Expo 86 and renovations made during that era. The colours lingered in public places like unwashed glasses after a New Year's party. The sounds of the Emergency room faded as someone wheeled me along, the hall seemed to narrow and surrender those dated hues as we approached an older wing. We stopped at a set of orange fire doors, beside a window looking into an office.

From here a nurse emerged with a clipboard. She wanted to know if I still felt suicidal.

"No," I said.

"And why did you try to commit suicide?"

"I'm a writer," I said, "and I've caused the end of the world."

"Oh really!" she said.

She sounded cheered, as if this was just the sort of thing she'd signed up for when she began her career in psych.

"It's just that we get a lot of a certain kind of patient in here," she said. "A lot of repeats. Your problem is a little more interesting."

"Glad I can provide a break from the usual, at least."

Michelle said something meant to reassure me and hugged me before leaving. Doors opened, the nurse wheeled me inside. I had been here a long time ago, as a visitor, though I didn't remember it at that moment.

I didn't resist being checked in. I could think of no better place for me, and expected and accepted all unpleasantness. It seemed dark, and getting darker. We went almost to the end of the single hallway that extended from the main area, into a room with two beds.

"All you have to do right now is rest," said the nurse. "Do you want to take off your jacket?" She helped pull it off, and I slouched onto the bed.

"That's right, just lie down." There was nothing else to do. I was probably already asleep while she hung up my jacket.

YOU KNOW YOUR LIFE has changed when you wake up in a psych ward. There is the time in your life before this moment, and the time after. Things about me would be measured from this episode on.

The room was bright. The other bed was empty. I lay fully clothed from the night before and wondered what to do next.

"Rise and shine, Jan!"

A different nurse. Short brown hair. Or a cleaner? No, no, a nurse. She wore a pale green outfit.

"Come on, Jan, time to get up."

We hadn't even been introduced. I rolled out of bed and stumbled after her. The floor gleamed and light streamed through windows. She walked ahead of me, occasionally looking back. "Come have breakfast. This way, Jan. Come along."

I followed her past other rooms. Showers. In a laundry area stood a large stainless steel rack holding stacks of folded towels. Then the main part of the ward. The double doors I had entered through the night before were in the far corner, beside that office with the big glass windows. Several more nurses stood or sat inside the station today, and from there they had a view of the entrance, the hall I had just walked down and, directly before them, the lounge. Chairs were pulled in and out, cutlery and plates remained on some tables, but most of the patients had already left the eating area. Somewhere a TV spoke. Many windows let light into the lounge, and I guessed that it was still morning. I couldn't say what hour it was.

"Here, why don't you sit right here," said the nurse.

She brought over a thick plank of blue plastic and took off its lid. Breakfast.

"Do you like peanut butter or jam on your toast? Or honey?"

I was not sure what to say.

"We keep orange juice and milk in here," she said. I heard a fridge door opening and closing. She brought a glass of juice. Really, I was sure she had better things to do. The health care system strained at the seams, from what I understood.

Alone, I ate a few bites of toast. I tried not to look in the direction of the other patients. Over my shoulder, people worked in that office, nurses in white. I couldn't see anybody watching me. After I had eaten a little, I returned the plank to a nearby cart.

The ward was in the oldest part of the hospital. The Expo 86 colour scheme didn't reach past the double doors. Brickwork, speckled floor tiles and brown carpeting predominated. Two large clocks showed different times. Potted plants sat under lights near two more doors. This exit led to a concrete pad and a fenced courtyard. I had probably driven down the road beyond many times but never considered this wing of the hospital. Which direction did I face? I couldn't guess which way Emergency might be.

The door opened to a room I hadn't noticed before and a tall man wearing a suit emerged. He put a hand on my shoulder. "Would you come speak to me, please?" I followed him into a second, smaller office, kitty-corner to the station, blue polyester drapes pulled across its single shatterproof window. He sat down across from me and introduced himself.

"I'm Dr. Brophy. And you're 'Jan.' Is that a Dutch name?"

"Danish."

"Let's talk about why you're here. Do you know why you're here?"

"The suicide attempt, last night."

"Why did you try to do this to yourself?"

I was silent.

"You told the nurse that you believe you've caused the end of the world."

I shook my head.

"You don't want to talk about it?"

"I don't think I should tell you."

"Anything you say here, I assure you, will be held in confidence."

I rubbed my forehead. "What did you say your last name was?"

He repeated it. "Brophy."

"Brophy ...," I said. "I went to high school with someone ... Mark Brophy."

"That's my nephew."

"What's Mark doing these days?"

"He moved to Winnipeg. Became a physiotherapist. Two children, a lovely wife."

"Oh good."

In junior high, his nephew and I had been in several classes together, and he'd struck me as someone whose experience of life was strictly regimented by a Christian upbringing. How different was the uncle? Something about his hairstyle and choice of suit suggested not very. The colour of his tie was part of it. Later it would seem odd to me that a devout Christian would pursue a career in psychiatry, based on my notions of both and a suspicion that somewhere along the way, in training or in practice, the tenets of one must clash with those of the other. But at that moment, I tried to decide how much information he could take and, having inferred much about his background, whether it was wise to inform him that within the last forty-eight hours, I had gone from being an atheist to deriving, on paper, an equation that proved the existence of God, and that I was an agent of his incarnation as Shiva.

I said, "You're a religious person."

"Yes."

"Has it ever occurred to you that all religions, Christianity, Hinduism, Islam, all of them, they might be part of one? That they all touch on the same thing? That they might just be different ways of trying to describe one great cosmic spirit, of which we are all a part?"

"Well ...," he said. "I suppose there are different ... *planes* of religion."

"All part of one."

"What does this have to do with you?"

It had to do with a book. I tried to explain the chain of events that it was about to set off, culminating in the end of the world.

"Did you say *your* book?"

"Yes."

"A novel?"

"Yes."

"But how will people see this book?"

"It's being published by Harcourt Brace in April."

"Oh. Really?"

"Yes."

He frowned.

"May I have a piece of paper and a pen?" I said.

A diagram would make it obvious. Many entities factored into the catastrophe I had set in motion — Harcourt Brace, Russia, the United States, the publisher of *Writer's Digest*, the magazine for struggling authors, India of course. I fit their names into boxes, linked them with arrows and notes to explain the action each would take against the other, the chain of events. Then, at the root of it all, me, me and my book. I thought I had given myself enough space on the page, but found myself writing smaller as the diagram approached a corner.

Finished, I handed the paper to the psychiatrist. I watched as he looked it over. Would he want me to walk him through any of the stages? Explain them in detail?

He raised an eyebrow, and he set the paper down sooner than I expected.

He put his fingertips together and took a moment to formulate a response. "Here, we don't like to say what will or won't happen in the future. I don't know if what you've described will happen or not — I can't say. But people come here, into the ward, with all kinds of things going on in their lives. The best we can do is try to help them find better responses to these situations. Better ways to view their own lives, and the stressors in it."

This was not the response I had expected. I shut up. Nodded at whatever he was saying. I had told him too much.

WITH OUR MEETING DONE and no indication of what was expected of me, and not wanting any more conversation, I sat in another chair and decided which patients I should avoid. Most sat in the lounge. Several were middle-aged women who appeared quiet and sedentary, and them I could tolerate. No problem, so long as they didn't speak to me. But one chattered away. I checked over my shoulder as she met a nurse.

"And how are we feeling today, Ruth?" the nurse asked her.

Ruth was saying, "— doesn't matter what time of day it is or how much traffic is on the road or how many people are waiting to cross and shouldn't someone write a letter to the people in charge because it's a hazard, a real hazard, I've seen children trying to cross the street and they won't wait long, children are impatient —"

She stood about as high as a fence post and her grey hair fell unbrushed around her face. She wore a housecoat and slippers and dragged her feet as she ambled about, pausing for opportunities like this: someone to listen. The nurse waited for a break.

"— it's only a matter of time before someone gets hit and then I'm going to have that on my conscience because I saw it could happen and I didn't do anything about it and someone should really —"

"Okay, Ruth, but you don't have to worry about that right now. Okay? Why don't you have a seat and try to relax?"

The nurse turned to another duty. Ruth shuffled on. Still talking. The topic hadn't changed, though the listener was gone. Would someone else hear what she must say? I was glad she moved slowly, as this gave me a chance to get up and take another seat whenever she approached.

Then, a familiar voice. I looked over my shoulder to see Michelle at the nurses' station, where someone pointed me out for her. Seeing my wife here startled me. I hadn't expected to see her ever again. She hugged me and set down a black nylon bag. Part of our wedding luggage.

"Mom and Dad say hello; they're thinking about you."

"Oh. Thanks."

"How are you feeling today?"

"Much better," I said. "Really a lot better. Things got out of control last night."

"I'm glad to hear that. You slept all right?"

"Yes."

"And how are you with ...?"

"I let things get out of hand. The situation isn't as bad as I thought."

"Oh good."

"Really, I think I'm okay now."

"I brought you some things from the apartment. Clothes mostly, your robe, your toothbrush. A notepad and pen, in case you want to write down your thoughts. I had to leave your electric razor with the nurses."

She rummaged through the contents of the duffel bag.

"Mom and Dad sent this along for you."

She took out a mason jar full of purple liquid. I rubbed my forehead as she unscrewed the lid.

"I'll get a glass," she said.

I kept looking at that jar and the thick, fragrant liquid it contained. Michelle came back from the kitchen with a Styrofoam cup, and I felt as if my blood had left the upper half of my body. I watched as she poured the thick drink.

"Here you go," she said, holding the cup to me.

I took it from her. Placed it on the table before me, carefully. I looked at the froth.

"Will you feel better if I drink this?" I said.

"What ...?"

"Please." I closed my eyes. "Don't ask me to do this."

"What's the matter? It's just grape juice. Mom and Dad thought you —"

"I can understand why they, and you, would want to do this. I understand, I really do. But I don't want you to do this. Please."

"I don't know what you're talking about, Jan."

"It may be better to let me live."

"*Let you live?*"

"I ... may be useful in the future, to the government. As a bargaining chip. They might be able to use me as a bargaining chip —"

"A bargaining chip? What do you mean?"

I looked away from the cup. The purple liquid.

"Poison," I said.

She stared at me, her mouth open. "It's only homemade grape juice. Just drink a little."

We sat.

"I'll drink it then," she said, and reached for the cup.

"*No!*" I grabbed her forearm. "No ... Please, don't!"

She pulled back her arms. Tears appeared in her eyes. The cup remained between us. "It's grape juice. We just thought you'd appreciate something from home."

I looked at the jar. Indeed, at our wedding, we had drunk juice extracted from grapes that grew on her family's property, bottled by her parents. It often appeared at special dinners. But here, at the hospital? A jar from home? Sealed, and resealed? Because undiluted, the juice had a thick flavour that could mask that of any chemical poured into it. I could understand why Michelle and her parents wanted me dead. That made sense: they had figured things out now, based on my suicide attempt, knew I had set into motion a chain of events that would end in a great conflagration, and that they, being the closest people to me, would bear the brunt of the outrage from the general public and world at large as disaster approached. They understood, and they wanted me dead, perhaps as a way of defusing some of the anger. I could understand that, I really could, but *should* I let them do it? Cosmic ramifications were very much on my mind, and I was unsure whether I should let them go through with this, because killing me would have repercussions, too. I didn't know. Dilemmas like this had ensnared me many times during the past two days and I often found myself unsure. I looked at the cup. Michelle's eyes were red and she took out a frayed Kleenex from her purse to dab at them. I should let her decide, at least.

"All right," I said. "If you really want me to drink this, I will."

I took the cup. I paused, with the Styrofoam lip at my own. Drank. I finished it.

"There," she said. "Do you want more?"

"I'll just go lie down now."

"Are you still tired?"

I nodded.

"Don't forget your bag."

Poisoned, I took the duffel bag, maintaining the charade, and made my way down the hallway. In my room, I didn't bother changing out of my clothes, just lay atop the bed with my hands folded on my chest. A suitable pose for someone about to slip away from the world. How long would it take for the poison to circulate through my body and begin disrupting vital functions? What would I notice first? Would it be painful? Would it start with a seizure, and end with me curling into a ball, face frozen in rictus? I accepted my fate, but I did worry about what might happen to Michelle and her family as a result. Not be prosecuted for my death, hopefully. Maybe sleep would be the first thing. Felt drowsy again ...

A couple of hours later I woke. Unpoisoned. I sat up.

Maybe it had been only grape juice.

Could it be that Michelle didn't want me dead? That she and her family did not know why they should want me dead? Didn't know *yet*, anyway ...?

I looked at the duffel bag. Inside I found my toothbrush. Clothing, a robe. As Michelle had said, the staff had taken my razor, which was electric and could not likely be used to off oneself, but needed to be checked by hospital maintenance people. Funnily enough, if I wanted to shave before then, I could get a disposable razor from the nurses' station, which seemed like an odd thing to hand out in a psych ward. Getting the blade out of its hard plastic casing would not be impossible, but what I had told the doctor and nurses was true, I had no desire to make another attempt at my life. Such things were no longer mine to decide.

I unpacked the notepad and pen. For writing down my thoughts.

I placed the two items on the small table beside my bed and paced within the room, considering what to write.

Should I tell people? Try to warn them? So they might prepare themselves for the disaster?

I began. I wrote down some of the realizations I had arrived at during the hours before my admission, and desperate advice I wanted to give to the human race.

When finished, I reviewed my work. The same problem occurred to me now as had during my discussion with the psychiatrist. My thoughts — and these writings — were dangerous. I didn't know what they would lead people to think or do. Did I have the right to put on paper my momentous revelations? What might result from these notes? What would people do with the knowledge? Would they be led into cosmically wrong behaviour? Did I risk worsening a catastrophic situation?

I should get rid of this page.

I smiled. I couldn't let them see that what I had written disturbed me. I was alone in my room, but had no doubt that a camera was located here, somewhere. I tried to look for it surreptitiously; I didn't want them to see that I looked for a camera. Better that the staff not know I was aware of its presence. Wherever it was.

The bathroom should be safe.

Discreetly I tore off the page and carried it into my tiny washroom. Even in a psych ward, they couldn't get away with putting a camera in here. That would be too much of an invasion of privacy. With the door closed, I commenced tearing the sheet into smaller and smaller bits, and held them over the toilet bowl.

Except. Except that the ward probably had provisions for this. No, the people in charge couldn't film patients inside a washroom, but they were probably quite used to them trying to flush revealing personal documents down the toilet, which could clog the plumbing — bad enough — so the builders had probably installed some kind of trap, out of sight but easily accessible by the same maintenance staff currently examining my electric razor, and they could recover sodden bits of paper, dry them, reassemble them, find out just what was so important that I would try to dispose of it in this fashion. This was likely one of the most effective means of information gathering available to the staff. So I sorted through the confetti in my hand and selected the bits that were darkest with pen strokes. I didn't need to swallow all of them, just a few key sections so that the soggy mosaic of my thoughts could not be put together in a meaningful way. I ate the paper. The rest went into the toilet. I flushed it, and emerged from the washroom with what I hoped was the demeanour of someone who had just satisfactorily voided his bowels.

The pad remained.

Anyone who had read a few books about spying in his youth, as I had, knew that what was written on such a pad could be recovered after the page was gone, simply by placing a piece of onion paper atop, angling a pencil lead against the surface and brushing back and forth until the indented words revealed themselves.

I sat before the small table again.

What, I wondered, might staff expect a psych patient to write on his first day in the ward, following a suicide attempt?

So happy to be alive! I wrote, pressing very hard, leaving no chance that the old indentations could be read. Lucky I was a novelist — I could imagine what a grateful-to-be-alive patient might write.

That solved the problem as well as possible. I wouldn't repeat the mistake.

But similar writings existed elsewhere. Looking at the pad, I now remembered where my volatile information remained. Carts

of blue plastic planks had been wheeled into the dining area and
I went for dinner, not feeling hungry, not hungry at all, digesting
my note and thinking of my Hotmail account.

IT SURPRISED ME TO SEE Michelle back at the ward. Whenever she
left, I thought, *That's the last time I'll see her.* She would put it all
together and realize that she (and the rest of her family, and
everyone who knew us) was safer if she stayed away. But she kept
returning, and I almost fell down with joy every time at the sight
of her. I no longer thought she wanted me dead. The grape juice
had been a misunderstanding on my part, I realized, and I couldn't
deny that my suicide attempt seemed to upset her. She was on
my side.

"Can you please do something for me?" I said. "It's very, very
important."

"What?"

"You need to log in to my Hotmail account."

"I've been checking our e-mail."

"This is different," I said. "It's an e-mail account on the web."

She didn't often use the computer. When we received e-mail
from family and friends, she usually looked over my shoulder
to read it, and she never used the word processing program
or played solitaire. In 1998 Hotmail remained something of a
novelty.

"Do you have a piece of paper?" I asked.

"I brought you that pad."

"I'd prefer not to use it."

She got a piece from her purse.

"Step one," I wrote. "Press the big round button to turn on the computer."

I wrote down each part of the process. What was simple to accomplish in practice made for a page full of convoluted instructions. Even I didn't like how they looked on paper.

"James," I said. He had been my friend since kindergarten: we could trust him. And he was comfortable with computers. "James can help you."

"But I don't understand," said Michelle. "Why is it so important to get into your ...?"

"Hotmail account. I sent an e-mail to myself. I did it during the day, before my shift at the library. Please please please, you must do this for me, you have to make sure that that e-mail is deleted. No! Print a copy first. Then delete it."

I squeezed a few more steps onto the page.

"Print a copy, but promise me — promise me — you will not read it." I told her to put it in an envelope and seal that envelope and give it to her sister Shannon. "Tell Shannon to hide it and not look at it. Somewhere nobody can find it. But where she can find it, if necessary. Because it may be useful in the future."

I had composed the e-mail shortly before leaving for my shift, knowing that after my death, as the world slid toward cataclysm, intense interest would focus on me, author of the book and author of the doom of the world. The message contained suggestions for rebuilding civilization, as well as my proof of the existence of a universal cosmic spirit, and I had hoped at the time that it might help populations around the world get through the coming calamities. Now, however, I was unsure. What right did I have to try to influence events? Who was I, *really*, in all of this? I could not trust myself. I couldn't trust the actions I had taken, and so I wanted that piece of information deleted before anyone cracked open my account and found it. Having a paper copy of the e-mail might be useful, though. When the first signs of my apocalypse appeared, Shannon could produce the letter and it might be used to prove my terrible prescience. Authorities would see that my predictive powers were real. They would take my warning seriously, and perhaps, just maybe, an effort could be mounted at the highest levels of international diplomacy to prevent catastrophe.

"I'm feeling much better," I told Dr. Brophy. Michelle and I had gone into the office after she put my scrawled instructions into her purse, and I tried to look relaxed and sane. "Things got out of hand. I had gone so long without sleep, I think I was overwrought."

"And what about your thoughts?" he asked.

I admitted to feeling some lingering concern regarding the publication of my novel.

"You've become over-anxious about it," the psychiatrist said. "You've lost sight of what a great accomplishment this is, and you're punishing yourself instead of celebrating, which is what you should be doing. You," he said to Michelle, "must remind him of what a great thing this is for him to have done. I mean, a novel! Being published in hardcover, by a major American publisher? I'm certainly impressed. I want to —" He lurched forward, and made a gesture toward my feet.

Kiss my feet? *Kiss my feet?* I smiled at the gesture, but secretly found it unsettling. When the things I had foreseen started to come true, and violence escalated across the world, toward its destruction, Dr. Brophy would remember me very well and understand that I was the instrument of end-times, and he would also remember that he had knelt before me, however briefly, however much in jest, and that small act would not sit well with him. What would he make of me, in coming days? Would he think of me as the devil on earth, stepped out of the Book of Revelation?

"How much longer," I said when the conversation was wrapping up, "do you think I'll have to stay in here?"

"Not too long, I wouldn't expect. We'll want to see that you get some rest and that your sleep patterns have returned to normal first."

I wanted out as soon as possible. I wouldn't sneak out, because that would upset Michelle and she shouldn't suffer my presence back at the apartment. But I couldn't be much use in the ward. I couldn't *do* anything, I couldn't attempt to stop what I had set in motion. There was no computer access here. No, I had to be discharged to pick up where I left off, and somehow attempt to correct matters, or at least try! Before Michelle left the ward I reminded her about her task, and afterward I wondered. Did I leave a *second* e-mail on the web, to be discovered? On a different web-mail account? I might have done so during that last shift at the library. Things were still hazy ...

I could not stop thinking about the e-mails and the doom of the world. In my next entry in the pad I made no mention of them, because I felt certain the staff would discreetly read these notes. The problem of the e-mails was mine alone to think about, and I did so through the day. At first the thought of going to bed was a relief, as I no longer risked conversation. But as I lay there, I continued to think of the messages and to wonder how much they had exposed me.

Would I be eliminated, in the night? I listened. No singing marksmen tonight. The weather had worsened, the wind rising and shaking the window. Outside, shadow trees whipped against a baffle of translucent blocks. Someone screamed.

Inside the ward — a man. Shrieking. A wall kicked. "You bastards! Bastards! Don't you touch me!" Obscenities. The ruckus came from another room.

My sleep had been severely disrupted in the days leading up to that final shift at the library and my admission here. I had lost my knack for sleep, in those evenings and unending nights, as I had tossed and turned, envisioning my doom, the death of everything. Down the hall somewhere, he continued screaming. *What were they doing to him?* The psychiatrist had mentioned sleep as part of my recovery. I knew that I had to do it, just fall asleep as I had a few thousand times before. But whoever it was kept thrashing, wailing, crying ...

It seemed to last for hours. Finally I got up and put on my robe and walked down the hall, and the shrieking got louder as I passed his door. The screamer's room was close to the nurses' station. A staff member must have entered at that moment, because the door swung, and I saw that this room, unlike mine, this room had no bed, no furniture, just padded blue mats on the floor and walls, like those we had used for somersaults in elementary school. Did I also see a strap? A buckle ...?

I went to the nurses' station. "Um, hello."

She looked displeased to see me.

"What's happening to him?" I said. "Why is he screaming?"

"Jan, I can't discuss other patients with you."

"But is he ...? What's going on in there?"

"You should go back to bed."

"I've just been lying there. I thought maybe you could give me something. For sleep."

She frowned. "I'll call the doctor in Emerg and see what he says."

I sat in the darkened lounge, waiting. The windows showed reflected light and silhouettes from the ward, rippling with each blast of wind outside. Howling continued inside, as well. A male voice sounded behind me. "How long is it going to take?"

A uniformed RCMP officer stood at the station, talking to the nurse. I couldn't hear her reply.

"We would like to get it over with," he snapped. "We don't have all night."

A cop?

I turned back to the storm. I could see little but the frantic waving of branches in front of streetlights.

The nurse called me over to the station. "You can take this," she said.

I took the pill gratefully, a small blue one. Turning to the hall, I saw a battalion of cops. Ten? Twelve? They were all uniformed, standing in a circle and talking amongst themselves. Why were they here? Because of the screamer? It must have to do with the screamer.

I made my way down the hall. I had to walk past the cops, and they took no notice of me at first. Then a woman, short, her curly hair pressed down by a regulation cap, caught sight of me. She looked at me. Stared. She stared. She saw me coming and spent a long time looking at my face. When I had passed the group and looked back over my shoulder, I saw that she had turned, and *still* stared at me. A new recruit? Someone trained to study faces, in case the information came in handy later? Perhaps she was just practising, practising her surly RCMP face, or practising her skills at facial recall, or *maybe she thought I looked familiar*, had shown up in a memo faxed to RCMP stations, or ...

Why she seemed intent on staring me down, I couldn't tell. Whatever the reason, her glare ruined any hope of sleep or a rapid recovery. The pill dissolved somewhere in my belly, its chemistry passing into my bloodstream, performing its function, and I stayed awake.

I lay on my bed until the screaming stopped. The storm continued, making the hospital rattle at its seams, and I could not sleep. I looked at my jacket, hanging from a post.

The same jacket I had worn, arriving here. The very same one I had worn at the library. I got up and went to it. I reached into a pocket, dug around. I had been surprised that my clothes and belongings had not been searched in any fashion when I was admitted.

It was a fleece jacket, and caught in the fabric of the pocket, the nappy fibres clinging like Velcro, were several small white pills. For convenience during that final shift, I had shoved a handful of sleeping pills into this pocket so I could take them at the desk, without need of removing myself to the washroom. And here they were still! Here, where I needed them. In my psych ward room. How fortuitous. In the washroom I filled a glass with water, trying not to think of that woman's stare, the cops, the screamer, that room with restraints.

Why did she look at me like that?

ROUTINES OF DAILY LIVING

I believe I am cursed with the ability to see what I have been the instrument of and I'm setting it down now so it might serve some purpose for mankind. I wrote a novel called "Shiva 3000." Shiva, the Hindu god of destruction — the destroyer — is what I have inadvertently brought forth ...

As the instrument of this event I feel extremely confused. Mostly I am sorry and scared for my loved ones, whom I don't dare worry at any point earlier than necessary. I wish I could at least live long enough to see if what I have predicted comes true. For now I can only wait for my executioner (now I understand why prophets are slain because nothing scares people worse than someone who jeopardizes their material world) ...

I handed the printout back to Dr. Brophy. Again we sat in the small office.

"You recognize this?" he said.

"It's the e-mail I sent myself the day I came in here. The Hotmail message."

"Your wife thought I should see it," he said. "How do you feel about what's written here?"

"I don't like to look at it," I said truthfully. I had only scanned the lines but I'd seen enough for my stomach to tighten. "I was in a bad state of mind when I wrote that. I hadn't slept for days ..."

He put the page in my folder and I was glad to see it gone. Bad enough that the psychiatrist should see it at all. I had feared he would want to go through it line by line, assertion by assertion. I didn't want him to know any more about me and my realizations. As I looked at Dr. Brophy, I kept thinking about the surprise visit by the police the night before. When I had first arrived here, I had been less afraid of talking. Now I felt uncomfortable. I disliked the way the psychiatrist seemed to stare at me. Why did people look at me this way? Him and the cop? What did they know that they weren't saying?

"Are you still worried about what will happen with the book?"

I was terrified. But I had to appear level-headed enough for discharge. I couldn't admit that I thought most of what the e-mail said still felt plausible. On the other hand, people would see through too rapid a return to my senses.

"Well," I said, "I do still feel concerns about the publication. And reactions. I am slightly worried. But I don't think any of what I wrote in that e-mail will happen. That this is the beginning of the end of the world. That I am the instrument of that."

He didn't challenge me, just listened. I couldn't tell what he thought.

"And what about sleep? How did you sleep last night?"

"Fine," I said. *Once I found my sleeping pills.* "There was lots of, uh, activity here last night. Someone screaming."

"Yes, I heard from the nurses it was a wild night."

"I had ... trouble getting to sleep. I'm still having trouble."

"We can adjust your medication to help with that."

Dr. Brophy wasn't always on the ward. I had been here less than three days but I saw the pattern, him arriving in the morning and staying for an hour or so to speak with each of his patients in the office or in a patient's room. They perked up upon his arrival. They chattered about him and what he had said to them or what they intended to say to him. He always wore a suit and the atmosphere was somehow heightened by his presence. Whose turn was next? What did he say? When he and I met, the conversation usually went this way, with him checking in on my mental state and my sleeping patterns, and discussions of how to get better. "Healing the mind isn't like healing a broken leg," he told me. "You can't just put a cast on it and wait for it to mend." I was desperate for tips. I knew — I could feel — that my head wasn't right, and I badly wanted it mended. If wearing some kind of head-cast had been an option, something that looked like a plaster helmet perhaps, I would have gone for it, gladly! I listened to what he said, honestly eager, even while working toward a swift discharge. *I will get better. What I'm saying about the normality of my mental state will soon be true, even if it isn't quite true right at the moment.* I listened, and tried to pry from him an indication of when I might get out. He was reassuring but not specific. "You need to start getting back into a normal pattern of living," he suggested. "You should try talking to people. Opening up a little."

When I stepped out of the office, I heard a thunderous guitar riff in the lounge. Someone was watching MuchMusic's heavy metal hour, the volume turned high. This patient sat by herself, others having cleared the zone of sonic doom. *Talk to people.* Normalize my thoughts. At least I should be *seen* talking to people.

The woman sat slightly hunched and turned from the TV so she couldn't see the screen. The music found a home in her head, which bobbed forward and slightly to one side, behind the beat. Why didn't she watch the screen?

"Are you listening to this?" I asked.

"I like rock music."

"Maybe I can find a different music channel ..."

"Is it satanic?"

I checked. The band was Slayer.

"Well, yes," I said, "but —"

"I am not a Satanist!"

"I didn't —"

"I am not a Satanist! I am not a Satanist!"

"No, of course not, I just —"

A nurse beetled over before I could be any more help, turned off the TV and consoled the woman, who continued to proclaim her non-Satanism, rocking back and forth without looking at anyone. I slinked away from the scene.

I divided the patients of the ward into two groups. Damaged people, like the non-Satanic Slayer fan, were the majority. Most of them were women, stricken by their illness and of no harm to anybody but themselves. During my admission, they were the ones to whom the nurse had referred when she said the ward saw a lot of the same people. Regulars. I had no doubt that Ruth, the short woman who always shuffled about, was a regular. It seemed as if she hadn't stopped talking since the first time I'd spotted her.

"— I can tell the exact moment when a pot of water has reached the boiling point, when the water in the pot reaches 100 degrees, and when it's mostly bubbling, and I know I would not pour boiling water into a fish tank. It's not going to do any harm to tetras above 30 degrees, they are tropical fish —"

Much too talkative. I continued to avoid her.

I was twenty-nine, and only a handful of patients were younger than me. One, an attractive woman who couldn't have been much older than twenty, sat closer to Michelle and me, each time Michelle visited. Miranda — she seemed comfortable with us. Only her hair suggested that she might belong here, slightly wilder than a stylist could explain. Was a section of it missing? Also, she didn't seem to blink. Michelle made it a habit to say hello to her, and a few days after my admission, Miranda was comfortable enough to make nervous conversation. Maybe she, too, had been encouraged to interact with others.

"Hey you guys," she said. "Why are they saying that?"

"Who?"

She pointed at the TV. It was off.

"Saying what?"

"You don't hear those voices?" she said.

"I'm sorry," said Michelle, "I don't hear anything."

Miranda paled. Realizing, I supposed, where those voices came from. It must have been terrifying.

Toward the end of the week, a new patient arrived and immediately drew attention. He was always grinning, chatting, shooting the breeze, taking control of the television or just sitting down with a snack. His manner made him impossible to ignore. The police must have supplied this second type of patient. If they took people out of here, as I had seen them do, then no doubt — no doubt — they brought them in, too, men who belonged in jail, but some detail of their crime or unwholesome act had landed them in the ward. I wondered if many men like this jokey, I-got-it-made fellow tried to add a bizarre twist to their routines, in the hope of coming here. If you were used to jail or prison or juvenile detention centres, the psych ward must seem positively cozy.

"Miranda," he said.

I could see no damage to him, couldn't understand his presence. He reminded me of certain jerks from high school, how they could lord over a bus stop or a washroom.

He gazed at her from the couch, where he reclined. "Hey Miranda, wontcha talk to me?"

She didn't look at him, though she could obviously hear him. The most centred woman on the planet would have found his attention unsettling.

"Miranda," he said. He singsonged her name. "*Mir-ann-daaa.*" He wouldn't quit.

"Miranda, don't you like me? Don't you like me, Miranda? Can I come visit you later? Miranda?"

Nothing could prevent him from dropping by her room at any hour. There were no locks on the doors, and the nurses didn't come around too often.

I should confront him. Here is where I should have spoken to another patient. In another frame of mind, I would have gladly told him to shut up, but here, now ... I couldn't bear confrontation. My room didn't have a lock either, something I often thought of. Someone barking back at me could have put me over the edge. I left the lounge.

"That creep is putting the moves on Miranda," I told a nurse.

I got no indication that it mattered, which was infuriating. Someone like Miranda should not be subjected to that, to an advance from some lout who wanted an incident he could brag about later to a cellmate. Should such a thing happen in this setting? Was this good care? I was ticked, ineffectual.

But the next day he was gone.

I didn't see him leave. Maybe it was a prearranged transfer, or maybe the system had a safety measure in place after all. I knew that people came and went during the night. It was something I wished I didn't know, but it happened. People came, people were taken. I found it impossible to stop imagining.

IN THE EVENINGS, a woman whom I didn't see during the days entered the lounge. Other patients were away for periods of time when they visited with family, so her absences didn't seem noteworthy. Maybe she only spent nights here. She was plump and had auburn hair pulled back from her face. Conversation still troubled me, but I reminded myself that I was supposed to talk to people. When I gathered the nerve to speak to her, I found her pleasant. She could have been somebody's aunt. The next day, walking down the hall, I happened to spot her in a room, sitting on a bed. So — she did stay here.

"Hi, Angela!" I called.

Her response was muted. Didn't she remember me from the night before? Maybe she had changed her mind about me.

Later she reappeared in the lounge. I sat down beside her and found that her friendly demeanour had returned.

"I have this problem," Angela said. "I can't be around people. Crowds."

"Oh! You're —"

I knew of this condition, this phobia. I knew the term but couldn't think of it.

"I've heard of that," I said. "Want me to go away?"

"I'm okay if it's just you. But if anyone else comes in here or sits near us, I may have to go back to my room. Don't be offended if I leave. It's my problem."

Offended? It didn't matter to me. She was a considerate woman whom I felt okay talking with, one of the few. I hoped nobody would scare away my find! We talked in general terms about being here, and I was deliberately vague about my book. Angela seemed good at not asking for more details. When my notoriety grew, I didn't want her (or anyone) to have to admit that they'd known me. An easy explanation for my presence in the unit was simply that stress over the imminent publication of my novel had led me to a suicide attempt. No more info necessary. People believed this.

Angela told me her background. Before this had happened, she'd had a full-time job, working in a complaints department.

"Well," I said, "that explains it. I wouldn't want to face people again either if I had to listen to the complaints of K-Mart shoppers eight hours a day."

"No," she said, "that wasn't it."

"All those bargain hunters. It must have been stressful. The complaints department! How awful."

"It wasn't the job," she said. "Really, I don't know what it was."

I felt pretty sure that it was her job.

ANGELA BROUGHT HER COPY of *The Lion King* to the ward. The viewing of this movie became a small event, scheduled for a certain hour on Saturday evening, with all of the patients invited to watch. Up until this point in my life, for reasons of personal conviction, I had boycotted all things Disney, refusing to buy for my

34

niece any article of clothing or toy or garden tool bearing the image of Mickey Mouse and his ilk, and I took pride in the fact that the last Disney movie I'd seen was *The Black Hole* in 1979. But this was a new circumstance. I liked Angela, entertainment options were few, and if there was ever a good time to reconsider one's opinions and give Disney movies a second chance, it was while committed.

We shuffled into the meeting room at the scheduled time and a staff member wheeled in a VCR and television before turning out the lights. Bernard, the patient I avoided most actively, made microwave popcorn. I wanted no popcorn or any other foodstuff prepared by him. He sat on the opposite side of the room, and that was good. Would Angela be able to tolerate so many people in such a small space, even to watch her favourite movie? I didn't notice where she sat. The movie began and I tried to give myself over to it. Nothing appealed to me more than the idea of sliding into a life-affirming musical cartoon for the next ninety minutes and forgetting everything, everything. Defanged entertainment would be perfect.

The Lion King began with the establishment of an African setting, in the palette of an animated Africa. I was familiar enough with the premise to expect to see the lion cub, born to jungle royalty. A friendly stampede of animals halted before a cliff to behold this cub, proffered by a druidic mandrill. Elephants and zebras bowed respectfully. The congress of animals approved, ecstatically approved, of their future king. The muzzle-nuzzling of his lion parents suggested a level of affection at odds with my understanding of lion behaviour, gleaned from my favourite National Geographic documentary, *Lions and Hyenas: Eternal Enemies*, but who could complain about such a display of tenderness? Presently, in the voice of James Earl Jones, Simba's father explained to his son that yes, lions do eat antelope, but when the lions die they become grass and the antelope then eat the grass. I expected this theme of "circle of life" to resurface later in the story.

But. A distraction.

The room had a large window and nobody had pulled the blinds. I watched the trees sway outside; it must be windy. Lamps patchily lit the shrubbery and bushes of the courtyard. Were they out there? *Who was out there?* I couldn't see him. But I suspected his presence. Yes. He was out there again. Somewhere. The blinds in this room had been left open *deliberately*.

Most of the others watched the movie impassively, but Bernard sometimes laughed aloud. I would hear him laugh and take this as my cue to smile, glancing at the screen — a tower of animals blossoming to sing a chorus — as if I too found the scene amusing and appreciated its lurid good cheer. But my smile was fake. I had lost track of the story, concentrating on trying to spot *him*, wherever he was, outside. Should I pretend I didn't know he was out there? Was that a better tactic? Should I be surreptitious, glancing outside? How well could he see me?

Hysterical laughter. Hyenas. Onscreen loomed the skull of an elephant but hyenas laughed, emerging from the empty case of bone. The hyenas could hardly get out a sentence without giggling in pop-eyed hysteria. I grinned. But thought of him. Out there. Waiting.

Why didn't he just shoot me? Be done with it?

The wait was excruciating. Not knowing when the shot would come was the worst part. Perhaps he wished to avoid shooting one of the other patients accidentally.

I got up and took a chair away from the others. Separating myself, putting myself in front of the window, an easy target.

Now he had no reason to delay. The blinds had been left open to make his task easier. That was clear. I had a poor view of the TV, but that hardly mattered. Simba bemoaned the death of his father. I could hear his confusion, sorrow, fear. He felt overwhelmingly responsible for a terrible turn of events, this ruination of his society, all the good things he had known, suddenly and irrevocably squandered.

I wondered if my corpse would cause problems. Would the medical examiner not want to touch it, knowing my identity? I, the agent of the world's destruction? Would he or she feel indescribably sullied by that experience? Would crowds riot outside his or her workplace? Would he or she be in danger? Would people fight for the opportunity to defile my dead body? Hakuna matata. Hakuna matata.

Hakuna matata! It means: no worries!

I worked at my ID bracelet. It was plastic and fastened with a device that made removal difficult without scissors. I worked at it discreetly. There would be no way to identify my body without the bracelet. James Earl Jones said, imperiously, "You must take your place in the circle of life." Why could the assassin not just shoot me and be done with it? Was it intentional, the wait? A kind of punishment? Another voice said, with distress, "Going back means I'll have to face my past!" But it was noise, meaningless noise. I could not and did not reframe my situation to see my imminent death by shooting as an opportunity to take a new place in the circle of life. No, my attention was dedicated to the courtyard and its many excellent hiding places for an FBI sharpshooter, and I thought of nothing but death.

Furious lion roars, infernal red light flickering across the faces of my fellow mental patients. I remained sitting, the plastic band on the tabletop. I stayed in place while Elton John queried whether or not we could feel the love tonight. Credits, presumably, rolled. The movie went silent. The other patients left the room.

No possibility remained of bystanders being wounded. I would let him have his clear shot. I took long breaths and held them. Take your shot, take it — just shoot! *Shoot!* There was no reason for him not to shoot. The walls glowed. It was the TV, flickering bright snow. Still I waited.

"Jan?" The night nurse opened the door. "Are you still in here? Come on, it's time for bed."

I sighed. Hadn't she been informed of the plan? Well, however this was being orchestrated, I could tell I was supposed to go to my room. Perhaps it would happen there. I stood up.

"Hey," she said as I passed. "Why did you take off your bracelet?"

"I couldn't stand to look at my name any more."

She nodded. "Fair enough."

THE ROOM WAS PLAIN. Cinder-block walls, painted a colour that would remind a person of nothing in particular, except maybe other hospital rooms. Two beds, though the other remained unoccupied. A place to hang your jacket. A small side table, and the heavy, mauve door to the washroom. Light flooded the room and made it seem white, white, white. As I lay, I could look at the white and almost think of nothing.

In the hallway I heard a familiar voice. "What's the problem now?"

"He won't get out of bed."

The owner of the first voice, a short man wearing a white coat and a stethoscope, entered the room. It was my GP, Dr. Fisk. I resisted the impulse to greet him. The psychiatrist followed him inside, looking slightly embarrassed. Oh well.

"Jan, hello, it's Dr. Fisk."

I nodded.

"The staff here have told me something upsetting. You won't get out of bed? Is this true?"

Well, I had also planned never to speak to another human being, but found it nearly impossible to hold out against a direct query. "It's not that I want to stay in bed," I said. "But I don't want to leave the room and come into contact with anyone else. I can't put anyone else at risk. It would be immoral of me."

"Why? What risk?"

"They'll be damned. Anyone I speak to. Even if I just go near them. I'm sorry, even you."

Dr. Fisk looked at me as if I had just sprouted rabbit ears. He had been my doctor since childhood; I'd never had any other, and he'd worked in the city long enough to remember my mother as a nurse. When he had removed a cast a year ago after I broke my hand playing soccer, Fisk had commented that the ER doctor used too much of the fibreglass compound, and I took this criticism of his colleague's work as a sign of our rapport. On other occasions he spoke of disliking Simon Fraser University enough to transfer to another school and program. That we had in common, although my choice had been the creative writing program at the University of Victoria — with terrible consequences, ultimately, for civilization, but that was something I tried to use the non-colour of the walls to avoid remembering. Little in our past acquaintance could have prepared him for such a conversation.

"You will not do anybody any harm by leaving your room and interacting with them," he said. "Believe me."

I smiled weakly. So naïve. But I wouldn't explain. Couldn't. Not when a chance remained for him.

"Dr. Fisk. If you would. I saw them getting another room ready. For me."

"What room?"

"By the nurses' station. One with padded walls. The police took away the occupant the other night. Please, if you could ask them. I would prefer not to be put into that room."

He shook his head. "You're not going into that room. You're not that kind of patient."

The two men moved toward the door, but before leaving, Dr. Fisk added, "Jan, you're going to have to let people here help you if you want to get better. You're going to have to trust them."

"I trust you, Dr. Fisk," I called. Dr. Brophy glanced back on his way out.

I lay.

Trust. Was that what they thought this was about? It didn't matter.

Would it help anyone, though, if I lay here silently and caused problems? Would this stop people from interacting with me? No, the staff would just come to the room, I realized. I had no control over who came and went here. People would be forced to come to me, and maybe I would ruin the life of someone who might otherwise have been spared. I didn't know. I didn't know, didn't know.

A nurse appeared at the door, the same one who had shown me around that first morning. "Will you please come have some breakfast?" she said. I didn't answer, but after she had vacated the doorway, I relented, got out of bed, got dressed and plodded to the lounge. She again played waitress to me, reluctant customer, and directed me to a table where Ruth and two other women lingered after eating.

"Cornflakes?" said the nurse.

I didn't answer.

"Cornflakes it is."

The flakes got soggy as I sat, staring out the windows of the lounge, at the bright day outside. The nurse left.

One of my tablemates was Dorothy, a pleasant patient, or so I considered her, as she rarely infringed upon my thoughts with words or actions. She hadn't spoken to me before, though she'd had time to get accustomed to my presence. "And how are you doing today?" she asked politely.

"Please," I said flatly. "I would appreciate it very much if you didn't talk to me. Any of you."

"Oh, oh, okay. Sorry! I guess you're having a bad morning. We all have bad mornings, don't we, ladies?"

"And stay back from me," I added. "Nobody go between me and those windows."

"Uh, okay, okay ..."

I watched outside. The courtyard. Bushes. Trees. Maybe the shooter waited for me to begin my normal routines before pulling the trigger, and so I began to spoon cereal into my mouth, my eyes switching from side to side to make sure that the ladies did not lean forward into the sightline of the rifle, or whatever weapon the assassin pointed. It didn't matter if other patients considered me rude. It didn't matter what they thought. I had hoped that these women might leave the table, but they lingered, and I listened to Dorothy yawn.

"I'm so sleepy," she said. "I slept so deeply last night. I don't know what they put me on, but I slept the sleep of the dead. Did you sleep deeply, too? Maybe they put everybody on the same thing."

People dispersed with the breakfast dishes. I ate my cereal without the interruption of a gunshot. Drank some orange juice. After waiting for so long, and having given the gunman every opportunity to do his work with minimal casualties, I had to admit that I did not know what factors affected the timing of my death. Maybe he didn't like to shoot someone facing him. I relocated, closer to the windows, and turned my back. Waiting.

The morning went on: other patients dropped into the sofa, watched TV or started pacing. Ruth began a discussion with a nurse. "I don't know who you've hired to do laundry but you can tell them that the only way to get a stain like that out of a towel is with bleach, a mixture of bleach and water, one tablespoon of bleach to a gallon of water, and scrubbing by hand ..."

In this position I had an excellent view of the nursing station, as well as anyone entering the ward from the hospital. I straightened every time the big doors opened with that latchety-click of the handle. Nobody of import.

And then, coming from the rooms, I saw someone I recognized.

Another physician, but also the husband of one of Michelle's friends. Actually, over time and social occasions, he had become my friend, too. He was a sharp fellow of Mennonite stock, as knowledgeable about Ernest Hemingway and Frank Lloyd Wright as about medicine. "Why do Mennonites disapprove of premarital sex?" he had asked me once. "Because they fear it will lead to dancing." From across the ward, he spotted me.

"Is that Jan?" he said, and made his way over.

"Hello, Carl."

He held out his hand and I shook it limply.

"I was just visiting one of my patients," he said.

"Carl. I'm sorry that you've seen me."

"You are? How are you doing?"

"Just ... sorry. Very sorry. I've caused a huge, terrible thing to happen. I know you will do this anyway but you must pretend not to know me, from now on. You never met me. Please. Just do that. For Nicole and for the kids."

His expression changed. "Well, okay." He looked at me a moment longer before standing and patting my shoulder. "You take care of yourself, okay?"

"Remember what I said."

He retreated. Left.

Poor Carl. How unlucky for him, to have spotted me here. He and his family would suffer for it.

I watched the staff. My suspicions fell and rose, irregularly. Could Dorothy have been right? Could the staff have given us all a heavy sedative? I had become ambivalent about the pills I was fed. Saturday afternoon I caught a large blue one under my tongue and proceeded to my room, where I spat it into the waste. Would nurses give out extra sedatives to patients, if it eased their workload?

I sat in the lounge until evening, when I heard the familiar clank and clatter. The noise of keys in metal cabinets followed the squeal of rusty casters, and patients stood up and walked over to form a line. I had quickly learned this routine, too, the med cart rolled out and noisily unlocked, the patients responding to the sounds like Pavlov's dogs to a dinner bell. A bedtime bell. I got in line too for my paper cup of water and handful of meds. I had no idea what I took; the names of the pills meant nothing to me. One evening I was being poisoned — "This will be the end of me,"

I remarked to a nurse — but more often I was just eager for whatever faint help the medication might offer. My prescription got bigger after the morning I refused to leave my bed, the new assortment hardly fitting in the palm of my hand. I gagged easily, there was no way I could down all of these. But I also thought, what's the difference between choking to death on pills and taking sleeping pills to kill yourself? I should be consistent, at least. If I was meant to die with pills lodged in my throat, so be it. But they all went down, easy as backgammon pieces.

The next morning I sat up in bed abruptly. The nurse who had shaken me awake jumped back.

I had been buried under an ocean of blackness and it was a challenge to surface — a zombie sleep, as I would truthfully describe it in my journal.

I had slept through the call for breakfast and the shrill bleating of my watch's alarm. I could barely write on my notepad. "Feeling so sleepy," I put down. If somebody hoped to put me to sleep for good, I would record my knowledge of it. My pen wandered. Usually my handwriting was merely messy; today it was nearly illegible. I tried to describe my torpor but the fact that the words strayed up and down over the page said enough.

Plodding into the lounge, I struggled to stay awake. I moved to keep blood flowing. My gait was stoned. I stumbled, stopped. Rested against a column. If I stayed in one place too long I would fall asleep, and as time passed I tried to watch the ward through a muzz of mental cobwebs. I had to sit down. I sat at a table, propping my head with one arm. Then put both arms down and rested my chin against them, drifting. The sleep that followed didn't feel nourishing, and anyway, I had already slept for ten hours. A slow whirl of static pulled me down, a gripping void, a non-place that waited for me to stop moving and close my eyes, a spotlight of stupor keeping me in its black beam.

Tea contains caffeine. Yes! I remembered this, as well as the fact that a good supply could be found in the kitchen, where — and this was also handy — the staff could not see you from their station. I stood and dragged myself over and plugged in the kettle. I picked a Styrofoam cup from the middle of the stack. I always used a Styrofoam cup rather than a mug, preferably one from a package that I myself had just torn open, and always from the middle. When the water boiled, I rinsed the cup before putting in the teabag, and I waited until the liquid had steeped to the colour of a pitcher's mound before forcing myself to drink. After the inevitable trip to the washroom, I prepared another cup.

After the fifth or sixth time, a nurse approached. "Jan, what's going on?"

"Going on?"

"You've been in the kitchen five times since I started my shift. How many cups of tea have you had today?"

"I'm just. I'm sleepy. Having trouble staying awake."

"So you're drinking tea?"

"Right. To help stay awake."

"If you're having trouble staying awake, you should tell me." I blinked at her.

"Look," she said, "you have to tell me these things. Today I'm your nurse, and I can't help you if you keep secrets from me. Okay?"

She was small-boned and long-haired. Short. She was about my age and did seem genuinely miffed that I had not confided in her. Could she be an agent of a secretive federal agency? It seemed unlikely. Maybe she was going along with the plan, maybe she had been kept in the dark about it, but whatever the case, I had a hard time imagining her doing anything to deliberately distress me.

"I heard someone saying. Everyone's feeling sleepy. I thought I was being ... *managed*, with a sedative."

"You received a heavier medication last night, to help you sleep," she said, "but we would never 'manage you' with drugs. We don't do that. I'll speak to the doctor about adjusting your meds tonight, so you don't feel like this tomorrow."

"Okay. Good. Thanks."

"But you've got to tell me these things. All right? Will you do that? Talk to me?"

I said that I would. I felt better, having spoken to her. And I was sick of tea. She was someone I could trust. Probably.

But her string of shifts ended that day, and the next day she was not in the ward: someone new was assigned to me, and I wondered, why? Why the change? What did this new person know? Who was *she*, really? A question mark would remain beside each new nurse until I'd decided one way or the other, and usually I couldn't decide. Worse, that night a male appeared in the nursing station and he didn't interact with any patients. He just sat back there behind the glass. I'd never seen him before. Moustache. Didn't look like a health care worker. *Who is he? What is he doing here, all of a sudden?* I spoke to a nurse, also sitting in the station.

"Would he please just get it over with?" I said.

"Excuse me?"

"I know who he is." I pointed at the moustached man in the background. "Him. Tell him to take me now."

The nurse rolled back on her chair and spoke to the man, saying something I couldn't hear. The unidentified man in white would not look at me. I couldn't hear what they said. He shook his head. Then, to me, she shook her head. No. He will not arrest you. He will not reveal his true identity. He will not give you the satisfaction of admitting his role. He will not look at you. He will decide the time. You do not talk to him. You do not see his eyes.

I stepped back from the station, watching them.

I went to a nearby chair and sat and tried not to stare. Familiar thoughts of doom cycled through my head. I checked. The man remained in place. Meanwhile, someone came to my table. The person in the ward I least wanted to speak to — Bernard. He was the reason I chose Styrofoam cups over mugs and rinsed them in boiling water. Bernard often ranged about the ward, dragging his right foot behind him. The foot seemed reluctant to follow, like a tin can tied to the bumper of a car, but didn't prevent him from moving about, and I viewed him as the alpha male of the place, though he didn't dominate by bluster. A nurse would come every other day with a blood kit and she and Bernard would repair to the privacy of his room as he made a cheerful joke, dragging his reluctant appendage. I imagined blood to have settled in that foot and made it a blue-black loaf with bulging toes. I avoided him. I avoided him in a way that I hoped would not be obvious.

Sometimes, Bernard's kids and a woman (perhaps his wife) would visit, and the smell of microwave popcorn filled the ward as they sat on the couch watching TV together, a happy family, or Bernard would get a pass to leave with them for an evening. Once he came back chortling about *The Rugrats Movie*, and how crazy about it his kids were. He tried to explain the characters to nurses in the station. "There's this baby, right? And Phil and Lil. Oh sheesh, you should see Phil and Lil."

He appeared very relaxed, as though the ward were a second home to him. "We're out of oj," he might inform a nurse, while peering into the fridge. "Probably want to order more apple juice, too." Smiling. Got along with everyone. Why, then, did he disturb me? It was his ease. His comfort made me wary. If he functioned so well in life, if he felt so pleased with himself, if he could care for himself, what brought him here and kept him here? He must be hiding something. Something worse than that foot. That foot. That foot meant corruption. This was not *The Canterbury Tales*. I disliked it when writers from Chaucer onward used physical shortcomings to suggest character flaws, but in the ward, this device worked in me. I judged Bernard, harshly and irrationally. The best I could do was try to hide my suspicions and avoid him. Now, when all I wanted to do was monitor the moustached agent in the nursing station and think quietly about the coming apocalypse, Bernard sat with me.

The lighting was too dim for me to see his face fully, just a few teeth in his smile and a curved gleam defining his hair. He seemed conjured.

"You live around here?" he said. "All your life? I'm from Kelowna originally."

His story came without prompting. Like Angela, Bernard had worked in retail, selling eyewear. In the Okanagan Valley, Bernard had had a life, a real one, a good one. But he had met someone new, and together they had ruined it. "I started seeing a prostitute," he said, and he seemed almost to be smiling.

Bernard said that he had blown everything on the hooker, and on motel rooms and drugs consumed in motel rooms. He lost his job, his house, his savings. I said nothing in response. *Don't let him know who you are.* A quick glance at the station. *Don't let him know about the book. Don't breathe a word that would suggest what you are and what you know of the universe and your role in the world's destruction. How might he abuse my secrets?* The only safe response was none. But the less I responded, the more Bernard seemed compelled to fill the silence, going into details of his downfall.

"... but she didn't know," he said, "she didn't know ..."

Why tell me this? How did the end of the world, for which I was catalyst, relate to this person? I didn't want to hear what he told me. Images filled my head. Drugs, prostitution, seedy rooms with crispy bedding and generic paintings of lighthouses on the wall. What did he want me to say? Was he deliberately provoking me? Was he, too, an agent? Or an example? Was I being shown why the world must be destroyed? Was that it? Was this my explanation? Should I let Bernard know that his day of judgement swiftly approached? As he spoke, that grin remained on his face, a half-grin. I imagined an old car moving slowly through some dusty side street in Kelowna and rolling to a stop for a woman wearing knee-length boots and a fake leather micro-skirt. Unpaid bills on a kitchen counter, the envelope torn open and the bill put back inside so the address no longer appeared in the cellophane window. A fight, a screaming wife. Bernard back at work the next day, gently putting a pair of glasses onto a customer's pleased face.

If I found myself genuinely wanting a cup of tea, I would gaze at the stacks of nested Styrofoam cups and wonder what prevented Bernard from secretly taking one from the middle and running his tongue around the rim before replacing it? Nothing.

Our conversation ended, finally, with him disengaging from me. I didn't know how to interpret Bernard, and so I had responded to his monologue with only noncommittal noises. But always, I watched him move through the ward and avoided the places where I thought he might go. My uncharitable theories of him ran rampant, damning theories, which all reduced to: *He is corrupt, or an agent, and I want him to stay far away from me.*

Of course, I did not share such thoughts with Dr. Brophy or Michelle. They might think I was still delusional. They might cite this as a reason why I should stay here longer.

THE PAY PHONE in the middle of the ward seemed to be ringing all the time. It would ring and ring, endlessly, and though it was only a few feet from the nurses' station, they never answered it.

Dr. Brophy suggested that a key to my recovery was the return to normal activities, to routines. The setting made this somewhat difficult. There was a list of duties that, during my first ward meeting, Bernard divided and assigned among the patients. When the meeting concluded, the higher functioning among us swarmed out of the room in a flurry of plant-watering and straightening-of-the-games-shelf. Bernard accomplished the most, quickly and efficiently, watering plants with his free hand held out to the side, almost daintily, his right foot lying askew behind him.

Ruth wandered about with a potted ficus in her hands. "I need to go outside into the yard where I can properly dispose of these leaves, these leaves are dead, the brown ones, and dead leaves must go, that's the first rule of plant propagation, get rid of the dead leaves and shoots so the rest may flourish, there'll be new buds and new leaves and the whole plant will grow better, and I need to do this outside, and —"

I found myself firing up a vintage vacuum cleaner and taking it to the faded carpets in the lounge. Weren't we violating some union contract, doing this work? Oh well, it didn't matter. It really didn't matter — despite my intense efforts, the grime and dust bunnies remained on the carpet, simply getting groomed with the passage of the machine's rollers. A male nurse remarked, "I don't think that thing works."

Neither did I. But I wouldn't let that stop me. Oh no! This malfunctioning appliance was the means of my recovery. I thrust it back and forth. It was working, I hoped, in a way invisible to the human eye. I could sense no immediate therapeutic benefits to my labours, but nonetheless made sure to diligently assail that section of ward carpeting between the office and the nurses' station, where the people who held my charts had an excellent view of me.

I learned that the nurses refused to answer the pay phone. I could just imagine the staff meeting where that decision was made. "I've got enough to do without being a receptionist for these people ..." The phone must have richly irritated them, ringing and ringing so close to their office, yet they never went to it. So answering the phone was a patient duty, too. I made it mine. Whenever I was nearby I would hop up and answer it.

Sometimes the person on the other end would start talking without the pleasantry of a greeting. Or they would ask for someone I hadn't heard of, and I would roam about the ward, trying to determine who was who. "Barry McGillis? Barry? Are you Barry? Do you know if Barry McGillis is still a patient here?" By the time I got back to the phone, the caller had sometimes hung up.

I would look at the phone when it wasn't ringing, too.

Before entering the ward, I had been involved in increasingly desperate discussions by e-mail with Michael, the editor of my novel — desperate on my end, at least. He was the only person, of anyone I spoke to in the period before my admission, who made the correct diagnosis: *You're going nuts.* A perceptive fellow. But there was one particular issue, a crucial one, that we'd been in the middle of debating just prior to my coming here. My book — the book that would cause the end of the world — was at a late pre-publication stage, and he had needed a decision from me, immediately or sooner. I hadn't given him one, and now I'd been in the ward for almost a week. I had assumed that my wife or one of my doctors had communicated with Michael, and that as a result the book had been cancelled. To my amazement, this had not happened. All Michelle had done was send him a brief e-mail saying I was "sick," with no more information. Much later I learned that because the book was the core around which my delusions had grown, nobody dared do anything, unsure how I would interpret any action. In hindsight it made sense, but at the time, I couldn't believe that my editor had been left hanging, wondering.

Nothing prevented me from phoning him.

Michelle had supplied me with a phone card. I remembered the name of the company my editor worked for in Manhattan. It would be a simple matter to get the phone number, dial, be put through to him. *Michael, you won't believe where I'm calling from ...*

But it had been suggested to me that I not speak to him yet. Not right away, not while I remained in what I myself knew was a highly imbalanced mental state.

So I just walked past that pay phone, a dozen times a day or more, waiting for it to ring or waiting for whoever was on to free the line, as I returned to the routines of daily living, extremely anxious.

The obvious solution was to get discharged. To demonstrate to Dr. Brophy that I was healthy again — which I would be, soon.

The things I professed to him in his office would soon be true, I felt sure. I knew that a big difference in the perceived sanity of someone lay in details such as whether or not he had showered, shaved and changed out of his pyjamas. Sane people attended to their grooming, whatever the challenges. My nighttime medications included enough sedative to tranquilize a pro wrestler. Michelle had brought me a travel clock, and I set its alarm to sound very early. When it rang, I felt as if yanked from a trough of medicated unconsciousness, an oceanic rift of nothingness where my personality wanted to stay, lying inert, unknown, unproblematic. But I would rise, alarm bleating, and rub my eyes until I felt awake. I would grab my toiletry bag and my electric razor — now with a sticker affixed to its side, blue letters stating that the maintenance department had examined the device and approved it for use — and I hurried down the hall to the lone shower for men.

"Plenty of hot water left!" Bernard reported cheerfully, emerging from the shower wrapped in a towel. I watched him lurch past me, dripping all the way down the hall.

I got through the door. I stood at the threshold of that steamy tiled enclosure. I wore sandals but was still reluctant to put a foot on the ledge. The shower walls glistened. The space was hot with water and Bernard. Did bits of Bernard float in the puddle before me? Maybe if I somehow turned on the shower and let it run for five minutes first ...

No, no, I couldn't. I could not make any kind of physical contact with the fixtures or surfaces or the water that would bounce off the shower walls. I went back to my room and settled for a vigorous facial scrubbing plus a generous application of Speed Stick, hoping that this would pass for cleanliness.

I received a pass from the psychiatrist to leave the ward, with accompaniment. Michelle checked me out at the desk, stating the day and the time when we expected to return, and signing a waiver saying that she took full responsibility for anything that happened while I was away.

We lived in the Fraser Valley, east of Vancouver. Leaving the hospital, we drove through the suburbs and into farmlands that had always influenced the character of the place. Why had I not appreciated this scenery more, before? The cedars, the fields, the buckled country roads. Being out of the ward, even for an hour, was such a huge relief, everything was great, just great. That filthy slough with scum floating on top was so great ... During the first of these furloughs, we simply drove, me sitting in the passenger seat like an elderly relative who used to be the one who did the driving but had had his licence revoked for the safety of the masses. We looked at houses, commented on which of them we liked or didn't. Michelle and I had postponed several things, buying a house among them, because for some time my highest priority had been leaving this city, which by my accounting had seen our residence far too long. But now ... well, now I could see us buying a house. Michelle had a good job with a sympathetic boss. I did too, actually, though I no longer felt employable. We passed a house with two small windows on the second floor. Perfect — I could board up two small windows. Paste newspaper over the glass, maybe. We could buy a house here with a second floor with few windows, and there I could stay to while away the days, like the madwoman in *Jane Eyre*, a latter-day Bertha, a docile male version of Bertha, grateful for his opportunity to be locked away, out of sight from humanity, sitting in a windowless room where he could do no harm.

And Michelle, my faithful wife, my unaccountably supportive partner who wanted me to enjoy myself when I was allowed out on longer passes, she ordered pizza as I liked it and rented movies and took me for walks by the river. I was happy just to return briefly to our apartment, where I could shower without thinking of a stranger's dead skin cells dripping from the tiles, and boot up the computer to ensure that certain messages had indeed been deleted from my Hotmail and Yahoo accounts, and look furtively at *our* telephone, for a change.

Then I would be returned to the ward.

In the Fraser Valley, November was a dark month. Rain dominated the weather; we had little snow through fall and winter but lots of rain, and on days it didn't rain, cloud cover would probably remain in place, a low, grey ceiling. The mountains darkened the area, too, delaying sunrise and hastening dusk, and when night fell I could feel anxiety growing in me. Night exacerbated my condition. If, before dark, I happened to spot someone in coveralls on top of the roof of an adjoining building, I knew that in a few minutes he would take out components of a rifle from his "tool kit" and discreetly assemble them behind the air-exchange unit. I knew that staff in the ward had passed along word of my colossal transgression to authorities, that the RCMP had alerted agencies in the States, and that these agencies employed people who could eliminate such a problem. As the courtyard darkened and streetlights went on in the distance, it became more difficult to see what was going on out there, but my certainty grew, I knew that the assassin preferred darkness to complete his task. I waited for him to do his work.

The television in the lounge went out. Every channel, static.

"That's weird," one of the patients said, flipping to no avail.

"It won't come back on," I said.

Because he'd cut the cable. The agent had meant to cut power to the ward but had severed the cable line by mistake.

"The lights are next," I predicted.

A clank and clatter from the nurses' station. Patients got up and walked over for their evening pills, the nurse unlocking the metal cabinets of the cart. Afterward, the others went to their rooms, for bed. I remained in the lounge, tapping a foot, staring out the window. *Just get it over with. Why wait?*

An older nurse wearing big glasses emerged from the station. She sat down near me. Not too near. Out of arm's reach. *Good.* She spoke in a manner that, to her, must have seemed soothing. She tried to convince me that going to bed like the other patients was a good idea, the best idea, would be best for all concerned. I kept checking over my shoulder, trying to see through the windows, outside.

She looked, too.

"What's out there?" she asked.

I didn't know what to tell her. She again glanced outside, following my stare.

"Are you ... are you expecting someone?" she asked, her voice trembling.

Eventually I went to my room. But didn't sleep. Couldn't. I lay on the bed, blinking. Time passed.

Around 2:00 a.m., my door cracked open. Light played on the wall ahead of me. The beam of a flashlight.

The person with the flashlight opened the door wider and leaned inside, carefully. A police officer. He aimed the beam of light up my bed, until it found my face. He stood there, keeping the light on my face while that nurse peeked inside. She wore a long sweater and held the collar closed tight around her neck. Noticing that I was awake, she waved and gave me a smile. Very fake.

I waved back. They retreated and let the door swing shut. The police were here again.

They came and went. They bided their time until they would seize me, inject me, drag me to their hidden room. They would punish me for the novel and the things it was going to do. The police were here on the ward, the nurses were their collaborators.

I was as crazy as when I'd entered this place. Worse, maybe.

PART TWO

The View from Peggy's Cove

A CAPSULE REVIEW

I HADN'T ALWAYS been like this. Certainly I'd never been checked into a psych ward before, and no incidents had hinted at the possibility of this happening one day.

Although ...

An asterisk remained beside my grade twelve algebra final in 1987. It was the provincial exam, which counted for half of my grade in that class, and the first of several exams worth fifty percent of the marks to appear on my transcripts. Algebra was a strength of mine. I had no doubt that I would score highly on the test, and it was my least concern among all of those scheduled for the week. Prior to being let into the gymnasium, though, I staggered to the washroom. I felt like I had to throw up repeatedly. I could barely stand, I felt so sick. Friends of mine had recently gotten food poisoning on a lunch outing, but I had been spared and they had recovered by this time, so it seemed strange that salmonella should strike me now. I shook, barely able to hold a pencil. But the exam wouldn't wait. As unfair as the circumstances might seem to a teenager, I would have to go ahead and take it. Feeling sick and cold, I sat at the desk and worked at the problems; a teacher gave me a pill of unknown identity and I soldiered through the two hours. Afterward I told people that the episode was my share of virus, and the next day I felt better.

Test anxiety is nothing new: I'm sure history is littered with examples of people getting sick before job interviews, driver's exams and toasts to the bridesmaids. But this wasn't my record and I had complete confidence in my algebra abilities. It made no sense that my body should respond in a way so contrary to what I knew in my head.

As a child I had gone through a hand-washing phase. Had we lived in the time of *Oprah*, my frequent trips to the washroom might have drawn suspicion and snap diagnosis from my parents or one of my older brothers, Erik and Peter. I was discreet, however. Although certain I had touched something poisonous, I didn't want my parents to know about it, or about my attempts to sanitize my hands and save myself. No, I shouldn't alarm them. I didn't wear gloves in the house or refuse to pet my dog, so the obsession wasn't simply about keeping clean. And no pleasure accompanied the act: I just needed to do it. Maybe I was careful not to be noticed because on some level, I knew the behaviour was abnormal and didn't want it to become a topic of discussion. Or I didn't want to be prevented from performing my duty.

The compulsion went away. Why it ceased is as puzzling as why it began. Maybe its cause would show if I could go back and look at what else happened around the beginning and the end of it. I forgot about that special weird hobby until years later, when I heard it described as an obsession that many children experience.

A minor personal anecdote, not that interesting. And, since whatever troubles I had known in my sheltered life occurred during school years, maybe school could be blamed.

One afternoon, though, when I was twenty-five and undeniably an adult, Michelle brought home Subway sandwiches and I had difficulty eating mine. I couldn't seem to get my mouth around the whole thing, so I removed some lettuce in an effort to reduce the circumference of the sandwich. Michelle remarked on the chewiness of the bread, and I thought that might explain the difficulty I experienced with my mouth — chewy bread.

After lunch, I went out in the car to finish my Christmas shopping. The sun was low and bright, and I felt annoyed whenever I turned toward it. No amount of fiddling with the visor helped, and the light hurt. Later I realized the problem was that my right eye did not squint in response to changes in brightness.

I went home and reported to Michelle that I now had trouble forming words — I needed to concentrate and make an effort to produce certain sounds. My face felt slow, anaesthetized. I still thought I maybe only imagined the sensation, or was thinking too hard about movements that should have been automatic, or suffered from having slept with my head in an unusual position, so that my face had yet to wake properly.

Brushing my teeth before bed, I was spooked by my image in the mirror — when I tried to smile, half my face lifted and the other half hung like a mask. I was surprised Michelle hadn't noticed, and when I demonstrated, she started to laugh, a little hysterically. She was afraid of what it might mean, as was I, though I assured her it would be gone by the next morning. We went to bed and she dropped off. I found something else wrong. When I closed my eyes, or rather when I tried to close my eyes, the right remained open. It was like a stubborn blind. I got up quietly and went to the bathroom for further investigation.

My right eye did not blink with the left — it only closed with a determined effort, and then with a time lag. I looked like the guy from Radiohead. At this point I removed myself to the living room to consult a big tome rescued from my parents' home, *The Family Health Medical Encyclopedia*, which my father had consulted instead of going to a doctor for regular check ups. Michelle had mentioned something similar happening to a friend's mother, and sure enough, I found all the details under the heading of "Facial Paralysis" — difficulty shutting one eye when trying to sleep was listed as a typical symptom. What I experienced fit neatly into the entry for Bell's palsy.

I was relieved. Everything pointed to this, a relatively common affliction with no associated problems. The fear that I had experienced a mini-stroke or witnessed the first symptoms of a brain tumour diminished.

The only remaining problem was how to get to sleep. How could I sleep with one eye open? I shuddered at a mental image of myself lying in bed, snoozing with one eye staring vacantly at the ceiling. What if I rolled over onto a tack? But here too, *The Family Health Medical Encyclopedia* served me. As it suggested, I retrieved a roll of Scotch magic tape and went to work, taping together the lids of my eye as I might the flaps of an overstuffed cardboard box.

The next morning, after untaping my face, I found that the symptoms persisted. My mouth hung more slack, mouthwash splashing down my chin when I attempted to gargle, and all my words emerged slurred. I made an appointment with my doctor but at Michelle's urging decided to skip the wait and go to a walk-in clinic. One was near the salon where I already had an appointment for a haircut.

I had once got a haircut to better suit a new pair of glasses and now I wondered if I wasn't getting my Bell's palsy cut. In the mirror I increasingly appeared like someone institutionalized. Next to me, an older woman with hair in curlers suggested my condition was a result of "looking at too many girls." We laughed. But inside, I wondered if this might indeed be some karmic thing.

I liked the concept of walk-in clinics, so much less paternalistic than making an appointment with your GP for two weeks later than when you really, really want the diagnosis. This clinic looked somewhat shabby — more like a tanning salon. The receptionist was vaguely hostile, perhaps judging my character based on my slack face and overly blow-dried hair. In the waiting room I noticed a girl I'd once worked with at Safeway. I pretended not to recognize her, too.

Shown to an examining room, I sat enclosed by old freebie posters from drug companies, and realized how flimsy the walls were. I could hear what was going on in adjacent parts of the clinic quite clearly. I liked the sound of the doctor, who seemed friendly and helpful, and I recognized the voice of his patient, another Safeway cashier. "It hurts whenever I pee," she told him. I had always thought of her as a bit of a twit, and this was confirmed when I heard her telling the doctor, for no reason other than pride, that she worked three jobs. Her and her urinary infection.

The doctor made me do a few facial exercises and took my ear temperature. He agreed with my diagnosis — Bell's palsy — and prescribed the medication I had expected from my reading, prednisone. He had a soothing manner and I thought of him as the good kind of hippie doctor — in later years, reading the local paper, I noted that he was one of the few doctors in town who refused to participate in a work stoppage protesting salary and workload issues. He explained that a nerve in my face had rebelled to give me the vaguely felonious look.

The only surprise came when we talked about the cause. "It's stress," he said.

I almost laughed, thinking of how little stress there was in my life, compared to that of anyone who actually complained of stress. Someone who worked three jobs and felt a burning sensation every time she visited the washroom, she could complain about stress.

"Has anything been going on in your life?" he asked. "Anything difficult?"

"No, nothing at all. Well, I've been doing the probate on my father's estate, but it hasn't troubled me in any way."

He was not swayed. "There's no scientific reason for this to have happened to you. You have that prescription now, and your symptoms will probably be gone within the week. But I think you should ask yourself why this happened. What, inside you, caused your body to do this?"

THE FORESEER OF PLANE CRASHES

SWISSAIR FLIGHT 111 seemed different than disasters before it.

It was 1998 — two years after my brief facial paralysis, and just after my first taste of publishing success. On the news we heard that a Boeing jet en route from New York to Geneva had crashed into the Atlantic. This felt more significant to me, somehow, than prior airplane crashes. Maybe the difference was two tickets sitting on our bedroom dresser, for a trip to India Michelle and I awaited.

It wasn't a fear of flying. I liked air travel. In other people I considered a fear of flying to be no more rational than my wife's fear of cats. Really, was there any better thrill than watching the ground whip past your window as you accelerated up or down a runway?

I kept watching the news. The coverage of the crash provided copious details about the flight and speculation as to why it had been so horrifically truncated. A new entertainment system had been installed in the Swiss jets. The flight crew had dumped fuel in anticipation of an emergency landing. The pilots reported smoke in the cockpit. Boats had scrambled from small fishing villages in Nova Scotia to search for survivors. There were no survivors. Two hundred and twenty-nine, dead.

Soon I began imagining catastrophe occurring on our flight, at some point during the seventeen hours — almost an entire day — that we were scheduled to be over the Pacific. This provided more than enough time for something to go awry, and nowhere for a cautious pilot to land at any early whiffs of trouble. I could see the flight attendants hurriedly collecting cutlery and unfinished meals and hear their hushed, atypical comments to one another. I could imagine the cabin lights going out. I could feel Michelle squeezing my fingers very hard and see the expression on her face as she whispered a prayer. I could hear hysterical outbursts in other languages from my fellow passengers — I wouldn't understand what they shouted but would share the sentiment. And I'd take a moment to look around the cabin, and I'd think, This is it, this is what it looks like. And then we would begin our final descent.

I first noticed the change in my attitude toward our travel plans during my last shift at the library, before my vacation days started. I felt curiously unexcited about the end of work. Maybe I hadn't been working hard enough to feel sick of it? Walking to my car, I felt strangely glum. My co-worker Gail had asked why we had chosen to go to India, and I listed off the reasons, the same reasons I had given dozens of people before her. I loved India. I'd been reading about it for years and badly wanted to see it for myself. We'd heard great things from others who'd travelled there. Suddenly the reasons sounded hollow to me. Gail expressed her certainty that we would enjoy ourselves and mentioned the great hospitality of Indian people. But I woke up in the middle of the night. *Our flight was going down.*

Over the next two days, my concern about the flight intensified. I called my brother Erik, hoping he could douse my panic with some of his typical level-headed insight.

"Maybe it's not the flight you're actually worried about. Maybe you're worried about being there, in India, and you're projecting your anxieties onto the plane trip."

Michelle and I had read a great deal in our travel guides and had received advice from friends who'd backpacked in India. We knew to expect more challenges and culture shock than in Turkey, where she and I had honeymooned, but that experience — quickly going from intimidation and uncertainty to loving the place and the novelty of everything — was our model. Still, this trip would be different. Would we get sick? Of course: everybody visiting India got sick. I had started to feel, to know, that Michelle and I would be struck especially hard and quickly, because thirty-six hours of travel would separate our departure from Vancouver from our arrival in Delhi. Three planes, four different airports. All that time confined to aluminum tubes, sharing recirculated air that had passed in and out of the lungs of our fellow prisoners. All of this, following a week of twelve-hour shifts for Michelle as she struggled to catch up at work before her holidays. We would arrive in Delhi exhausted, sleep-deprived, infected. First we could expect unscrupulous taxi drivers to hustle us. We had a room reserved at the Y for the night of our arrival, but how would we get to the Y? Our taxi driver would find it so much easier and more lucrative to pull the Hindu-Muslim riot scam, as detailed in our *Lonely Planet* guide. We wouldn't get to the Y. And if we did, it would be a deathtrap. We would perish in a fire.

"Maybe," I said to Erik's suggestion. But I no longer believed we would get the opportunity to die of smoke inhalation in an overcrowded motel that lacked an emergency exit.

Coverage of the Swissair disaster reached what felt like a new level of media saturation, and my new phobia fed on an interview I heard on CBC. In it, the chairperson of an air safety committee explained her decision to resign, as a protest against the lack of meaningful improvement in the field. She supplied me with the counter-argument to that classic response to concerns about air safety: that flying was safer than driving. "It depends on how you measure safety," she said, "by trips or by miles." Like her, I now measured by miles. I offered this up to my brother. He didn't believe it.

The computer took my side, though. It was easy to find information on the web that supported my point of view. The best website had a comprehensive overview of airline safety, complete with rankings by fatal events, most fatal regions to fly, and thoroughly detailed accounts of dozens of crashes. What a resource! I went back to that site repeatedly, to estimate the chances of our jet arriving at its destination intact. Obviously, one should avoid any airline with Cyrillic letters in its logo, but should he also beware of those that had not yet had an accident, as they were coming due for one, statistically speaking? The nationality of the carrier was not a reliable indicator of safety. If you couldn't trust the Swiss to maintain a machine properly, whom could you trust? Based on my reading, it seemed pretty unlikely that *any* aircraft could leave the ground and return in one piece. And all that time we would spend flying over the Pacific, with thousands of acres of water below when we desperately needed a landing strip ...

I took further augury from the media. When Phil Hartman had been shot by his wife, I had had a premonition of real trouble for Bill Clinton, involving Hillary. This had happened, and now I learned that Roddy McDowell had died; to me, still recovering from a childhood devotion to *Planet of the Apes*, his death seemed another omen of my imminent demise. A leap, but I couldn't resist making the connection. When Michelle's parents said goodbye to us, the look in their eyes told me that they didn't expect her to return alive. Every parting felt like a last goodbye. We visited our friends Mary and Dave, and I felt grieved that we would never again spend time with them. I went for a hike alone up a small local mountain, which seemed an appropriate thing to do during one's last days on Earth. *Why haven't I gone on this hike more often?* Why hadn't I come here every day? Just a twenty-minute drive from our place ... Why hadn't I made an effort to enjoy this view, or the many other small pleasures around me? Why had I squandered so many opportunities to appreciate life? Well, too late now. Morose, I descended the trail.

Nights were the worst. We had bought mosquito netting to take along, and we practised putting it up and sleeping under it before we left. I woke in the middle of the night with the tack having fallen out of the wall, leaving us pooled in netting. I slept less and less as our departure date approached. I would get up and turn on the computer to check one more angle on the safety record of Malaysian Airlines. There was talk in the news of a terrorist of growing notoriety named Osama bin Laden, who had relocated to Kashmir and promised to wage war on India and beyond. Planting a bomb on a Malaysian aircraft bound for India seemed a wholly credible course of action for him to take. Anticipating the many hours we would spend on planes or sitting in foreign airports, we had borrowed one of those electronic travel games, poker, and I found myself already using it in my office, long after midnight, sitting against a wall, trying to use the icons of cards flashing upon its tiny screen to while away the hours and distract myself. How likely was it that our plane would crash? The air safety website supplied statistics, and if I recalled the formula correctly from my Logic 101 class, I could roughly equate the chances of midair disaster to the likelihood of getting a royal flush on the first draw. Then I only needed to hit the button for a fresh hand, again and again, until that set of cards came up. I was tempted to be spooked by the ace of spades, but, I reminded myself, I was not superstitious. No, no — I was rational.

And I would go back into our bedroom and uncover Michelle from her death shroud of cheap mosquito netting and wonder, What had I done? What had I done to her and her family? I lay back in bed and wished that we were doing anything else in the coming days, that any other plans for the next few weeks were ours. I could only fall asleep by telling myself, Don't go. Don't go! That was the simple solution, wasn't it? Just don't go. By contrast, what was the worst that could come of that?

When Michelle came home from her last shift before vacation, she told me how her day had gone and I broke down sobbing. Sobbing was new. She knew of my trouble sleeping, and that I felt unprecedented anxiety over the flight, but I had never before displayed this kind of emotion, this unflattering, debilitating fear. I couldn't regain control of myself. She poured me a drink from a holiday bottle of liquor, which seemed an old-fashioned way of steeling one's nerves, but I wouldn't argue. We were scheduled to depart the next day. We agreed that we would wait and see how I felt in the morning before making any change of plans. But inside, I felt the issue was already decided.

The next day, when we surprised Michelle's sister Shannon

with the news that she didn't need to drive us to the airport, I had worked up enough conviction, specious reasoning and vivid imagery that all three of us wondered if something awful might happen to that plane during its flight. We watched the news. I checked the web. But, nothing. Roughly thirty-six hours after my decision to chicken out, a jet safely kissed the tarmac somewhere in Delhi. I was not the foreseer of airline catastrophes that I had thought I was.

Humiliation topped the negative outcomes of not going. We'd told everyone our plans; now we would have to tell them of our hasty decision not to go, and what lay at the root of it. I felt hugely relieved for not having to get on that plane, but a different kind of queasy, too. A fear of flying? So we explained it to people, but was that really me? It didn't feel like me. Worse, it felt bad to have surrendered to the fear so wholly. I had been in a mental state unlike any I had experienced before, and the lack of control over my thoughts unsettled me. "I think I'm going crazy," I told Michelle's parents, when we startled them that weekend by showing up at their cabin.

We quickly booked a different holiday, as much to flee the people who might see us in town and ask us why we were not in India as to satisfactorily use our vacation time. We took a trip across Canada — by train. Didn't every Canadian want to take a train trip across the country at some point in his or her life? Judging by our fellow diners in the dinner car, it was something most people felt they could postpone until their golden years, but what the hell, we had friends to visit along the way and new provinces to discover. We should have been jam-packed inside a train chugging between destinations in India, with people clinging to the outside of cars, our bowels uneasy, every inconvenience

73

and unpleasantness of travel foisted upon us. Instead, we and our silver-haired travelling companions returned from the dining car each evening at 8:30 to find our beds made for us.

And after five days and four thousand miles or so, we got off in Halifax, Nova Scotia, and took a bus to Peggy's Cove, beautiful Peggy's Cove with its perfect lighthouse, apparently the most photographed thing in Canada. I walked past the lighthouse. The bus had wended through the small village, and we'd passed a dock still hosting boats from the Department of Transportation, uniformed officials walking back and forth in their Day-Glo safety vests. The recovery effort continued. This small harbour served as the centre of operations, close to that point on the ocean where the Swissair flight had gone down. I stood on the rocks and shielded my eyes, staring out at the water, trying to decide the general location upon all those waves where pieces of jet had rained. We were in Nova Scotia. Not Delhi. Because I had a fear of flying. Or something. I knew I would look back on this episode and wonder what it said about me; I already did wonder. *Was it actually the book?* From the waters, officials raked an amazing number of fragments of twisted aluminum, and in a hangar somewhere, experts would cobble together a reconstruction of the jet, a patchwork reconstitution of the entire plane that looked like some sculptor's nightmarish statement on the ills of modern society. But even with that done, even with the fuselage reassembled to show a gaping, obvious hole, it might remain impossible to say with certainty why the plane went down. The exact cause might never be known.

There is a section in a novel, *Flaubert's Parrot* by Julian Barnes, that I often think of. The book is about an amateur scholar interested in the life and works of the nineteenth-century French author, Gustave Flaubert. Much of the book concerns the protagonist's ideas of the author, trying to conjure the man's character from known facts of his life. In the section that struck me, Flaubert's accomplishments are listed year by year in capsule form. Reading this summary of happy events and significant achievements, one can only view Flaubert as a genius living a charmed life.

Then comes a second review of his life. This time, only the deaths around him and other negative episodes are recounted. Flaubert now comes across as a chronically ill wretch, beset by personal and public failures. In both lists the information is biographical; neither is a "truer" picture of the man.

This I've done to my own life, assembled a capsule review. First, the good list (not unlike what you'd send to your grad reunion committee for the *Whatever Happened To ...* booklet.) Then, the list containing just the low points of my life and most glaring demonstrations of character flaws, and a review of this one can pop any bubble of self-esteem. Try this yourself, it's a hoot! To useful outcome, I might have done the same thing with incidents in my life that I had starred as peculiar:

1969

Born.

1975

Obsessive hand washing.

1987

Strange fit before algebra exam.

1996

Bell's palsy, with undetermined inner cause.

1998

Near hysterical bout of fear of flying.

I might have looked at the pattern here and foreseen some-thing, really foreseen something, a small catastrophe over the horizon, waiting to be added at the bottom of the list. But I had other things to think about.

PREPARE TO MEET GOD

THE FRASER VALLEY of B.C. is a good place to farm. The fluctuating lay of the water that has run through it for millennia created huge tracts of good soil. The fecundity of the earth has attracted farm families from Holland, Mennonites from Russia and Germany, and, more recently, Sikhs from the state of Punjab in India. When I tell people I grew up surrounded by Mennonites, I'm often asked if they drove horse and buggy. They didn't, at least not in my lifetime, nor did they wear big beards or broad-brimmed hats, or indulge in any other habits one might associate with the Amish. The most thrilling example of extreme Mennonite behaviour was a father throwing his son out of the house for having purchased a television, and this was only notable for its rarity.

The Mennonites and others did provide a tendency in the population — a feature in many agriculturally based economies, it seems — to be religious, and for religion to flourish like rows of corn. The Fraser Valley is B.C.'s Bible Belt. Beside a highway at the far edge of one field, a billboard reads: *Prepare to Meet God*. It's a chilling message to motorists heading toward the Fraser Canyon, where the mountainside drops away just past non-existent shoulders, and logging trucks come roaring down the twisting single-lane highway. The billboard has no accompanying heavenly graphic or attribution to put it into context, just black letters as stark as the advice. I liked to think it was a farmer who put together this billboard from scraps of wood, after he came up with a message he wished to impart to drivers. Prepare to meet God. It could be the catchphrase of a pious action hero.

An oft quoted but dubious statistic about our city was that it led the country in both small crimes and churches per capita. Certainly a house on a quiet suburban street could look like all the others until the day police cars arrived, and the cops busted down the front door to reveal that this was one more rental property husked by the newest farmers of the valley, 1,600 square feet of house converted to an indoor forest of marijuana plants and hydroponics equipment, with perhaps a corner of the kitchen still intact for domestic needs.

The crimes weren't always petty.

In our last year of high school, Michelle and I took a day job at K-Mart, as part of the inventory team. It must have been a Sunday, because the store was closed. It had not occurred to me before that K-Mart or whichever retailer could not fully rely on the numbers collected by barcode readers, but must occasionally pay people to touch and count everything that hangs from hooks, stands in pyramids, sits on shelves, lies jumbled in markdown bins. Walking through a fluorescent cavern has its challenges when you only want a tube of shoe glue, but imagine being a member of a motley group hired to touch and look at and record the number of every product contained therein.

We needed to learn specialized skills before the counting began, not just the procedure for recording our tallies on the preprinted tearaway sheets, but how, correctly, to write the numbers themselves. There was a right way and a wrong way to form each of the ten digits. A "4" should be written so that its top closed, and the protruding section formed a right angle to the vertical post. On none of our chits should a "4" with an open top appear. Only an asshole would try to pass this off as a four.

We began. I counted and counted and left behind my filled chits, like a Greek hero hoping to someday emerge from his labyrinth. Except that the white lists spread and multiplied throughout the store. I made my numbers in the prescribed manner. The novelty of the task faded. I counted tins of butter cookies and tubs of car wax featuring a cartoon turtle and blister packs of small fabric pads that would prevent furniture from scuffing floors. I was soon separated from Michelle, but little room remained in one's thoughts for talk, anyway. No muzak played and the announcement system was not used, because we concentrated. Nameless bags of potato chips. Boxes of garbage bags.

"Hey. Heyyy, guy."

It was the weedy fellow following me, one of the older-than-school-aged people in our group. He had a moustache and lank, long hair cut short in front. The procedure was to count everything not once, but twice, the second tally made by another person, such as him, who checked his result against what I had written on my sheets.

"Third time I found a mistake on your sheets."

"Oh. Really ...?"

My head ached.

"Yep. Thirteen bottles of Aqua Velva; you put twelve. Don't believe me?"

"I believe you."

"We're getting paid by the hour. You need to slow down, partner."

"Okay, sure. Thanks."

"There's no bonus for getting done early."

"Right."

"No need to hurry; might as well get the extra hour in our cheques."

"Okay."

"Take it slow."

"Sure."

"Might as well get the money, eh?"

"Yeah."

I went back to counting. Slower. How could it be any slower? Lemon fragrance plug-in air fresheners, salt and pepper shakers in the form of comic toadstools. The possibility of finishing early faded. Just telling time was harder after so much counting, and, with my knobby, ill-shaven, highly accurate counterpart trailing me, the work was both slower and tenser. Finally, at last, no pegs remained undecorated with a double-checked chit full of properly formed numbers: the contents of the store were accounted for, and I found Michelle and the two of us walked toward the doors, feeling not merely tired but punished.

"Did you hear the news about Jacquie?" someone, approaching from the other direction.

"No," said Michelle. "What news?"

"She's in the hospital. It's so awful, she's in the burn unit! Her mother is dead. She died, was killed — her brother tried to kill them all, in their house, they set it on fire! They set the house on fire with them inside!"

Jacquie was a friend of Michelle and her sister. I don't know what anyone said in reply, and what would it have mattered? Many people were closer to Jacquie than Michelle, and certainly me, but I knew her, she went to our school, I would have said hello to her if I'd happened to spot her here, and her brother had tried to kill her, by fire, had killed her mother ...? Such news was enough to make me throw up. But I didn't, I just walked in shock, we just said whatever we said and walked out under bright lights, fatigued, disbelieving, the numbers of dish soap and diapers still polluting our heads — how could this have happened *here*? To someone we knew?

DRIVE FARTHER DOWN the same street where a rental house has recently been eviscerated to make room for pot plants and you might happen upon another church, *yet* another church, one you hadn't known existed. The small community where I grew up supported no fewer than three mammoth churches. In town, they were uncountable. One of the more popular ones hosted sermons in the parking lot during the summer, for fun, and a joyful honking would rise every so often. But over the past decade, the need for a conventional church-like structure in which to worship had lessened, and some new congregations made worship in the strip malls that blighted the city over the same period. Today one might see parishioners file between a hair salon and a Subway sandwich shop to attend the Church of the Glorious Daybreak. The names hint at the breakaway nature of the new congregations — someone has a different spin on what worship means, and so starts a new church with others of the dissatisfied faithful — and if the splinter group is too small to lease a space where pets were once groomed, it might instead rent a high school gym on Friday nights. I pity the student forced to worship in the same place where he or she has also been made to grapple over a basketball.

It's a religious place even if you don't go to church. At one intersection, a number of roads converge awkwardly. The junction almost guarantees you will have to stop for a light, and you might find yourself, on a Friday night, stopped beside men and women of various age, waving signs at you. One person's bad urban planning is another's pulpit. Parishioners of new churches work from the sidewalk, waving cardboard signs at idling cars. "Are You Saved?" "Jesus Died for You." "Will You Be Ready When He Returns?"

The Book of Revelation is key to these people. A certain type of patron would come into the library with a wooden cross the size of a cobbler's hammer dangling from his or her neck, worn on the outside, this Christian coming to pick up a volume of the bestselling *Left Behind* series to enjoy more adventures of a group of citizens "left behind" by their spiritually superior family members — called up by the returned Saviour — and those people left behind must match wits with the devil while attempting also to upgrade their souls. I assumed that the books' readers — many of whom were adolescents — kept the series popular because they so enjoyed a post-apocalyptic adventure à la Stephen King's *The Stand*, but with the bonus of it being permissible Sunday reading.

An English professor at university told me Revelation was written when Christianity was threatened. It was an unsurprising reaction in the face of what looked like the end for the sect and its members; the faithful spun their oppression around and predicted the death and destruction of non-believers. Where I grew up, with Christianity under no threat, Revelation seemed to grow in popularity, continuing to provide a you're-gonna-get-yours appeal, and whenever a Bible was the only reading matter within reach, I would flip to the end for a jolt of seventeenth-century Stephen King. Like Bosch paintings, it's an acquired taste.

At high school, every three or four months a rumour would circulate that the Rapture was nigh. Some authority, no doubt operating out of a Bible college in a southern state, had studied the book carefully enough to determine the exact time that all those Christian corpses would leap from their graves for final judgement, leaving non-believers behind to deal with the guy with hooves. And here we were, getting advance warning! I had no fundamentalist friends, but such news spread from its source, reaching the Christians in our circle.

"Of course it's probably bogus," he or she would say, "it probably won't happen. But just in case. You have asked to be saved, haven't you? I mean, what's the harm? Doesn't take much effort, and just to be on the safe side, you might as well do it. I mean, who knows, right?"

The date would come and go with no sign of Jesus. And we would learn that the Bible-studier in Texas acknowledged that he had made a slight miscalculation, perhaps misjudging the length of the life of Abraham, or the exact time when the Israelites had reclaimed Jerusalem, and the date for the Rapture was resched-uled for exactly — *exactly* — three weeks later.

I had little to do with fellow high school students who might mark down on their calendars the date of apocalypse. But to my friend James I confessed a growing interest in a girl in our English class.

"Oh, her," he said, not without sympathy. "Good luck. Isn't

she religious? If you do go out with her, you won't be getting any."

She was somewhat religious. But he and I didn't make distinctions between different versions of Christianity, or appreciate that a broad spectrum of opinions could be supported within. This particular English student went to the United Church, and her opinions on everything from abortion rights to premarital relations were similar to mine. The United Church was the one I had abandoned — the very church that she still attended, that was the place I had avoided going, when I was a boy. Apparently I hadn't stuck around long enough.

Luckily, Michelle could tolerate my lack of churchliness. I maintained my case for scepticism, even atheism. I had reasoned it out and spent many an evening nurturing my position. Out of respect for her beliefs and an abiding desire to discover the practical limits of her liberalness, I mostly avoided the topic.

She awakened me to the mix of opinion within local religious groups, and told me that the fundamentalist congregations, which were in the majority in the Fraser Valley, held the United Church and its membership in some disdain — didn't consider it a "real" church. It was far too liberal, with its participation in nuclear disarmament rallies and advocacy of social change to eliminate poverty. When the United Church ordained its first gay minister, scorn reached such a level that some members of Michelle's congregation began looking for other, less tolerant places of worship. I was amazed. People really split hairs like that? They really cared so much about policies that they would bother to leave one church for another? I had assumed people picked a church based on the easiest drive and best parking. Who knew? Sometimes I wondered if she perceived a bigger schism than actually existed. On the other hand, she knew more people than I did, even had friends and acquaintances belonging to those other religious camps. Down the street, a man had fathered so many offspring that they were not merely children, but a congregation of his own making. Somehow the youngest, Debra, was permitted to befriend Michelle.

"I think he considered your family a mission field," Debra told Michelle later, relieved to be out of the man's sphere of influence. Among the prohibitions placed on her, she and her sisters were forbidden to wear pants, except on Sports Days at school, when she could wear pants under her skirt, and when he sent her up to the roof of the house to do shingling. There she stood after school, wearing her skirt and pants, hammer in hand, as her teachers and fellow students walked home on the sidewalk below.

My creative writing professors in university would have enjoyed seeing this kind of detail in the short stories I wrote. After getting my degree and returning to the valley, I could not convince myself the place had changed. I had changed. Now I was broke. Because my degree was in writing, I felt even less employable. I had lived away long enough to notice something else about the Fraser Valley that set it apart from other places — the surrounding mountains tended to trap clouds. It wasn't just the trail of the river that made the land fertile, but so much precipitation, twelve months of the year: in all of Canada, this city had the most churches, the highest rate of petty crime, and all of the rain.

THE BURN PILE

1995 WAS THE FIRST year of my life in which neither of my parents lived. My father had died in May and my mother predeceased him, back when I was in junior high. On New Year's Day Michelle and I were at the old house, sorting through a quarter-century of accumulated stuff while the estate was settled. That night, I woke. We were sleeping in what had been my father's bedroom — probably because it was the warmest room in the house, located above the woodstove. I got up and went to the window to look at the fire outside. Maybe the wind had woken me.

During the day, Michelle's parents Dave and Eleanor had come to help us sort through things that couldn't be given away or sold in the garage sale, resulting in a huge pile, the makings of a good bonfire. They had brought some of their own unwanted belongings, and the whole thing had seemed like a good idea at the time. "This is great," I had said during the day, looking at the fire as it crackled and breathed. "This should be an annual activity, burning unwanted things on New Year's. Get rid of your baggage! It's very symbolic."

It was a huge blaze that afternoon, and at 2:00 a.m., it continued. Looking out the window, I could see only the fire on a black canvas. The wind had risen, and as each gust shook the house a swarm of sparks streamed from the blaze toward the forest and the homes of neighbours. We had made the fire in a field where it seemed a good distance from everything else, and it was January, but suddenly I felt as if I had imperilled the neighbourhood, maybe the whole mountainside.

What a way to let the neighbours know I had returned! Up until my father's death, I'd been living with Michelle in town. I'd found employment through the Fraser Valley Regional Library, perhaps the one organization in the area that wouldn't see a creative writing degree as evidence of a character flaw. Much of the work resembled what I had done for Safeway to get myself through university, but at least at the checkout desk I'd be handling books rather than depilatories, diuretics and cans of corn, and I'd have reading in common with the people I served. I worked at a variety of branches, but one sat in the very town of my upbringing; in fact it was the same library my mother had taken me to as a child. I had been going to this place since it opened, almost twenty years earlier. I had taken copies of *Owl* and *Ranger Rick* and *Mad* off the juvenile magazine rack as they came into reach. The branch had a finite selection of books, but I discovered at age eleven that with the assistance of the librarian, the works of H. P. Lovecraft could be summoned. Then, for a time, mere literature interested me less than the travails of Laverne and Shirley, so I didn't need a library. Now I returned to this small branch as an employee and found the carpets unchanged. The librarian was also unchanged, except now she was "Gail" to me.

In truth I saw my raison d'être as writing. Oh sure, for a wage I would check out books to people wearing chunky homemade crosses, or stuff a thousand overdue notices into envelopes, or

tape the edges of scores of *Sweet Valley High* paperbacks to reinforce their binding and so prolong their life, but in reality, *in
reality*, I was a writer. Yes, a day would come when one of my supe-
riors invited me to join her team selling cleaning cloths of near
miraculous properties on a commission basis, but even if she didn't
comprehend my role as scribe, I did. Money I earned allowed me
to drop a shift here and there and spend more time working on the
novel. This I was good at, keeping to a writing schedule. I had read
that Stephen King wrote six pages a day, so in university I tried to
meet a similar benchmark. In addition to my course load and
whatever stories I had to write for class, I also wrote at least four
pages of my novel daily, sometimes working late, forgoing the
invitations of my roommate, who went out to enjoy his carnality.
"Doris Lessing is going to be speaking on campus next week," a
writing prof announced. "But her lecture is scheduled at the same
time as our workshop. Now, I'll consider cancelling the workshop
if everyone assures me they'll go to the lecture. Okay? Everyone
will go? Is there anyone here who won't show up?"

I raised my hand.

"Jan, you *won't* go hear Doris Lessing?"

"If the workshop's cancelled," I said, "I'll spend that time
writing."

He rolled his eyes. This belonged to the same category of
enthusiasm that made me wear a pen on a string under my shirt
for moments of inspiration away from the desk, and collect words
from my Word-of-the-Day calendar in the glove compartment,
for reading material at stoplights and car washes. I could probably include all of this in my list of early warning signs of mental
problems — who in university looked to Stephen King as their
role model? I should have been aping Kafka or Camus, anyone

with a beret. But I had picked up another chestnut of wisdom from *Writer's Digest* magazine or somewhere, to the effect that once you make writing the first priority in your life, everything else will fall into place. How true! Finally I'd found something I could be a zealot about. And it didn't matter if I moved back to my hometown, a city where video stores outnumbered bookstores twenty-five to one, because all I needed was a room to write, some free time, and money for postage to send out my manuscripts.

I knew not to be optimistic. Of the many graduates of the University of Victoria writing program before me, I only recognized the name of one — W. P. Kinsella — as a novelist. So, if over the past fifteen years the university had graduated an average of eleven people per year with a degree in creative writing, then the chances of that degree actually translating into publishing success hovered around one in one hundred and sixty-five. I could expect to remain anonymous. I had spent about two years writing my novel, and this realization lent its completion a melancholy air.

When I quickly found an agent, and when he quickly found a publisher, and the publisher was a large and prestigious one, Harcourt Brace, the surprise seemed shared all around. Through my agent, *Writer's Digest* asked me to write a short article on "Query Letters that Made it Happen!" This was intended to encourage people trying to break into print. I'd seen and read these pieces myself in the annual guides the company published, and I took it as an indicator of the rarity of my circumstances that now I was being asked to draft one. After learning of the novel's acceptance, I felt, for about twelve hours, a sense of immense gratitude, relief and accomplishment. I could phone family and friends and tell them the news, I had done the impossible, the whole "writing thing" was not just a pipe dream, it was happening. It was really happening. Michelle's parents were among the people I was most pleased to inform, as they had given me the most encouragement of anyone I knew besides Michelle herself.

"I suppose now you've got the hard work of editing ahead of you," said her father Dave.

"It's going to be fun," I said quite honestly. "It's all going to be fun."

I was keen to participate in every step of the process and find out what it was like to publish a novel. I didn't dread the editing stage, because I didn't consider my choice of words sacrosanct and was very comfortable editing my own stuff. I enjoyed seeing the improvements. Because nobody but me, my agent and the editors at Harcourt had read the manuscript, I also looked forward to getting the opinion of another reader. My editor Michael was the person who had persuaded Harcourt to accept the book, so I felt sure that he was a wise fellow with superb taste.

There was one small, minor, tiny problem. Minuscule, really. In actual fact it was the problem of my professors at university, not mine. In their view, you could only write a story or a novel if you were on intimate terms with the subject matter: preferably you had experienced the events yourself, and the resultant fiction was but a few degrees shy of creative non-fiction. So if my writing instructor took up rock climbing, it wasn't entirely because the mountain was there, or that he needed exercise. But this could be time-consuming, couldn't it? A year out of your life to get material for one short story? Or, in my case, for a novel that I wholly did not expect to sell? Perhaps what that older generation of writers failed to appreciate was the number of new resources available to someone like me. I was of a new generation — electronically enabled. I had every issue of *National Geographic* on CD-ROM, for crying out loud. My collection of reference books blossomed with every purge at the library, not to mention the fact that I had an insider's connection to the many resources available through my employer. And, of course, I had the internet.

This was a huge asset to people as clever and technologically savvy as me, this newfangled World Wide Web, delivering a limitless amount of information directly into your office, or guest bedroom, as the case might be. "Don't write about other cultures," my favourite prof warned. "And if you do — whatever you do — don't write a piece of fiction from the point of view of someone from a culture other than your own."

But what if you must? We had received a postcard from one of Michelle's friends, travelling through India, and it featured an image of a monkey-like figure pulling apart his chest to reveal a pair of illuminated lovers, and I knew this was the culture for me. I wanted to find out about India and write about it, because I wanted to escape the place where I found myself, the hometown I had been returned to. If I lived in India, well, maybe I'd recall my childhood home with fondness or curiosity and feel compelled to put something into words. That same prof had preceded everything he told us with the caveat that these were the rules, and once we had learned them, we could try breaking them. I was ready to break some rules! Break out on my own! Break the moulds! Wasn't that what a young writer was supposed to do? Strike out for yourself, brave new territory, follow your passions!

Still, though.

As with most of my professors' advice, this bit had an irritating way of sticking with me. I had to admit that I was not of Indian descent, nor a Hindu. I was a Hindu wannabe. But wasn't mythology the thing? The book I wrote was centred on the mythology, gods and goddesses like those featured on that postcard. It was a fantastical story, nobody would mistake it as literally true. It was just what interested me, and I had fiercely held onto another nugget from *Writer's Digest* or somewhere, that a writer should write the kind of fiction he or she most wanted to read. Well, *Shiva 3000* was exactly what I wanted to read, and I knew of nothing like it in existence. When I began writing the novel in 1996, my final hedge against my profs' warnings was that I knew to expect a lengthy delay between the acceptance of a manuscript and the final edited, composed book going to the printer. I could write what I wanted using available resources, and then, in the unlikely event of me actually selling the manuscript, I could quickly arrange for a trip to India to answer questions I might still have about the place, people, setting.

Now I had sold the manuscript. Most of my communication with my editor Michael, as with my agent, took place by e-mail. It was always a shock to hear a human voice, someone calling at 7:00 a.m. from New York, not having factored in the time difference. It startled me to see material evidence of the book's acceptance, as when a courier delivered to our apartment the seventeen-page contract with Harcourt. Seventeen pages ...!

"It's pretty standard," my agent e-mailed me.

Shocking, too, was the sight of the manuscript back from my editor.

"I don't think we'll need to make many changes," he had told me previously. I had replied that I thought the first few chapters started slowly, hoping that he would think of a way to pare them down. But when I flipped through the manuscript, I found it saturated with red pencil markings. There wasn't a single page where he hadn't found something requiring alteration. He didn't even like the last line! How could anybody not like the last line of the novel? "She would forget, and I'd tell her again tomorrow, and the day after, and the day after, however long it took when words had to substitute for memories."

It seemed unlikely — inconceivable, really — that anyone could find fault with that line. I had spent a lot of time considering the book's final sentence and, when I'd arrived at that one, knew I had found it. At the outset Michael had prefaced all his suggestions with a letter stating I could change any line-edits back to original form, and could ask for a different editor if I thought our views were incompatible. No, no, I definitely didn't want that, and of course I wasn't married to my text, but I nonetheless looked upon all these markings as stab wounds to my manuscript and wondered if they weren't fatal. I had been careful in arranging my words and sentences. My prof had suggested that a good thing to do before sending out a story was to read it aloud, so that you could listen for awkward phrasings as well as hear if your prose had the intended rhythm, the right balance of long and short sentences, a satisfying braid of stresses and meaning. Among the problems Michael noted, in that accompanying letter,

3. Absolute participle constructions ... my problem is that you drive the poetic device into the ground. Conspicuous overuse. So I tried to reduce its frequency.

In the manuscript he had fixed this. But, now, in addition to making the corrections, I would need to reconfigure the whole novel for rhythm, and spend at least one more weekend closed in my room, reading aloud until my voice wore out. I wasn't sure if my prof read his novels aloud, too, but I wouldn't omit that step.

Having access to an editor via e-mail must have been relatively new to the world of publishing, as well. Although we were separated by many miles, several time zones and a border, and had never met in person, I could ask for clarification on any small comment he had made in the margin and expect a quick response. If I couldn't bear to look at his response, I could opt not to connect to the net until the next morning, or whenever I felt steeled. It was convenient. And harrowing. I expected exasperated replies but received, through and through, thoughtful comments and encouragement.

I reprinted key sections with our amalgamated changes, to see how they would look on the page and how the result read. I lost count of how many times I read the entire manuscript. Twenty-five times? Thirty? I grew sick of it, and yet I couldn't stop going back to it. Further readings uncovered lines or phrases that had merely been placeholders, good enough at the time of writing but that I had intended to change, and lo and behold, I hadn't yet done so. Someone's expression was as "neutral as a staircase," because I couldn't think of anything better than a staircase to convey the idea of neutrality at the time. I still couldn't think of anything better. Neutral as a ... goat? As a bicycle? Or maybe a ... staircase?

Worse, each time I reread, I seemed to discover another detail that I had not double-checked when I first wrote it into the text, or something I had misinterpreted upon one reading and now knew, from more research, was wrong. A name that I had used for a male character was distinctly female. How deep was the river Yamuna, anyway? I had imagined the Fraser River as I wrote the section two years ago and had not considered the matter again until now. I would phone up a co-worker of Indian extraction and ask him for some obscure piece of information. I drove to the college library to pore over its reference books for one more detail and drove out of town to another library when I had exhausted that supply. When a necessary change presented itself, it often had a ripple effect, so that I had to go from start to finish of the novel working out all of the changes spawned by one early mistake. Edits consumed more and more of my time, and that feeling of accomplishment had all but dissipated. Perhaps this was the revenge of the creative writing professors. *Never write about a culture other than your own.* I wiped sweat from my forehead because it was summer, and also because it fit with the disapproval I imagined, for not having heeded sound advice. But I would do what it took. I could and I would. I wasn't going to blow this. Michelle and I went for walks, and I stepped quickly as I babbled about my latest unpleasant discovery.

The march to publication followed a set timetable. When I couriered the manuscript back to my editor with our combined edits, that should have been the end of it. But there was another stage. In a month or so, I could expect to receive the galley proofs of the manuscript — the newly edited work as it would appear when published. But I photocopied the edited manuscript before mailing it back to him, so that until those galleys arrived, I could continue to sift through the novel, trying to find anything else needing attention. Correction of the galleys should have been limited to minor errors in spelling or punctuation made by whomever typed up that red-marked mess, but I suspected that if necessary, I could squeeze in a few more minor adjustments if I felt they were mandatory. *If.*

There was yet one more stage before the book was out of my hands, as its text became closer to becoming fixed — bound galleys. This was the novel as it would look in print but soft-bound in a plain wrapper, complete with all edits, the copyright notice and the dedication, something to be mailed out in advance to critics, magazines and other authors from whom we hoped to receive a blurb. The bound galleys said Harcourt Brace on the spine next to the wavy divots that were their logo, and inside readers were warned not to reproduce the contents of the book in any fashion. The work then changed from an abstraction to something lacking only a glossy cover.

I badly wished to refrain from making more edits and breaking the covenant of non-changes — I didn't want to be the clichéd writer who makes himself a nuisance to his editor and publisher. But more and more online resources were coming into my reach. The library subscribed to a huge database of magazines and journals, and I could plug in a word like "sati" and get two or three articles to add to my reading. Also, my skill at searching the internet improved, a colleague having put me on to a search engine called Hotbot that was superior to the one I had previously used, and I could make it trawl the web for any word or phrase.

My sleep deteriorated. This felt very similar to what I had experienced nights before our recent aborted trip. I might get to sleep okay, but find myself awake at 2:00 a.m. For forty minutes or so I would lie and shift on the mattress, which had somehow lost its ability to give comfort. This felt like that night at the old house, me waking to see the bonfire outside, still burning. Now I thought of those galleys lying on my desk, the manuscript fattened by colour-coded Post-it notes I had inserted throughout. As with the bonfire, night made it seem much bigger.

Insomnia was not the novelty I had expected from television shows and anecdotal reports. It didn't make me feel like a tortured genius who had greater things to do with his time than sleep. There was nothing I wanted more than sleep. The few hours I got didn't refresh me. They lacked in those deep cycles that were key to rejuvenation, and gradually this became another thought to keep me awake. *Have I forgotten how to sleep?*

The only thing to do was get out of bed. In my office/guest bedroom, I glanced at the manuscript, but resisted going back to it. My old friend Electronic Travel Poker beckoned. I also had most of my books in here, carefully arranged on the shelves of a case built by my father. I had intermixed beloved trashy stuff with books that would display my keen intellect: anybody looking at these shelves could see that I was neither pretentious nor a philistine. No, I was some kind of Renaissance man, judging from the mix and its arrangement. I had put in a few books of poetry to demonstrate my sophistication: an appropriately tatty copy of Michael Ondaatje's *The Collected Works of Billy the Kid*, another by a former prof, Marilyn Bowering. The arrangement had been done with a mind to varying the colours of the spines, so that not too many dark ones sat together, looking like a clumsily collected series. It had been a lot of work, given how few people actually came in here to evaluate my character. I looked at these books and knew that none offered what I presently needed.

They interested me too much. These books might spur my mind rather than lull it. Besides, being favourites of one kind or another, they shouldn't be associated with this nasty episode and the knot in my stomach. No, as remedy for insomnia, you wanted a book to which you felt no particular emotional attachment. I considered Virginia Woolf's *The Waves*, a book that I still owned only because I thought it too cruel to inflict on an unsuspecting used-bookstore customer. But another requirement in a soporific is basic readability, so that your mind won't wander off the text. From Michelle's bookcase I took out and seriously considered *Leviathan* by Thomas Hobbes. It had given her nightmares in university, though — a towering redheaded philosopher had chased her through sleep after she struggled through a day of eighteenth-century intellectualizing. I put *Leviathan* back. I could afford no nightmares.

One of my profs, W. D. Valgardson, a B.C. author and long-time faculty member of UVic's writing department, had encouraged his students to build up their personal reference libraries, and from this subcollection of mine I finally made a selection. I had discovered that my employer regularly rid its collection of books whose cover laminate was peeling or whose spines had been broken or, I suspected, merely bore cover illustrations that suggested the work had been published in an embarrassing decade. The information within remained useful, and I liked the idea that someday I just might write a story for which I desperately needed to consult *Portraits of the Maori* or *A Collector's Guide to Porcelain Dolls*. It made me feel as if I had an interesting and varied publication list ahead of me. They were far from handsome, these books, and would never find a place in my other case, but with each book sale I had the pleasure of adding something like *An Introduction to Invertebrates* to my own little private library of discards. Sometimes I would peel off the library's tape and old barcode in an effort to rebeautify them.

The book I decided upon came from a Time-Life series called *The Old West*, but I had just one volume, *The Loggers*. Once, its physical attributes must have given the impression of luxury. The book was padded with a brown faux-leather, but with age this had come more closely to resemble the material that might upholster the dashboard of a 1978 El Camino. The tanned leatherette was tooled with motifs, scrolling patterns of a western theme, lariat, steer horns, a sunset, all surrounding an oval cameo that contained one illustration in colour, a pair of old-time lumbermen standing atop the bole of a mighty redwood. Hopefully I would join them in sawing logs — I judged this book to be very boring indeed. Given that the publisher was American, I could be assured that no references to the logging industry around the Fraser Valley would occur to pique my interest.

It did help the first night, but in the morning I woke before Michelle, and the next night I got up to find my place in the ongoing duels of lumber barons. The author had gamely tried to work human-interest elements into the history, but I found myself forced to reread segments to absorb meaning.

The men who filled the logging gangs and ran the sawmills of the far West originally came from all over the globe. In spite of their diverse backgrounds, however, as a type they had much in common: great muscles, insatiable appetites, the daring and drive to do dangerous labor for as little as $1 a day plus board and keep, and a penchant for booze, brawls, and bawds.

Booze, brawls, bawds: that should have been enough to keep a reader focused, shouldn't it?

Instead, I wondered about the lump on my back. It looked like an oversized vertebra and felt like a goose egg. Years ago Dr. Fisk had told me it was nothing to worry about. But now I wondered. I put aside *The Loggers*. The *Family Health Medical Encyclopedia* was not as helpful as previously, and I felt I really needed a definitive answer, at 3:12 a.m. Luckily I had my new research tool. I booted up the computer and searched the net, reviewing pictures of tumours and looking for the one on my back. But the closest match was a kind of cyst, and the internet too suggested I had nothing to worry about.

I still couldn't sleep. A few minutes after lying down, I again knew the lump was malignant, and that I was a fool for not having done something about it years ago, instead of letting it grow and spread roots through my body. My mother had died of cancer when I was fifteen. My having it too made sense. I remembered how my father had driven up the driveway. I had sensed real trouble because he and my mother's aunt had stayed at the hospital long past visiting hours. My mother's aunt drove up the driveway very slowly. My father followed at a normal speed, and honked. A honk. My concern was already sky high; I hadn't visited her that evening because I had a soccer practice. A soccer *practice.* So, when my mother was choking on bile or whatever, a Kinsman was throwing a soccer ball against my head and remarking on the bounce. I could tell from the two different styles of driving up the driveway that she had died. Tonight, I wondered how long my tumour had been metastasizing, and on what day I passed the point of any hope of successful treatment.

I tried lying on the guest room futon, thinking that a change of venue would increase my chances of dropping off. No. Next I tried the sofa in the living room. I turned. That lump was in the centre of my back, and I could feel the small yet distinct dimple it made in the cushion. I watched the venetian blinds. We lived in a corner unit condo that belonged to Michelle's parents, overlooking a farmer's field on one side, a mall on the other. Were streetlights getting brighter? Did a car sit out there, stalled, its headlights increasing in wattage? Or had the moon come out from behind clouds, with a sick, grainy glow?

No, it was just sunrise. A sickening dawn. A half-hour later, I heard the alarm bleating in our bedroom. Michelle was surprised when she came out to find me sitting on the couch.

"I'm going to see Dr. Fisk today," I told her. "I can't take this any more."

She was glad to hear it. Usually I was reluctant to make doctor's appointments. As soon as the office opened, I phoned.

"All right, Mr. Jensen," said the receptionist. "How about two weeks from Tuesday?"

"No," I said. "I need to see him *today*."

"Dr. Fisk has no openings today. I might be able to squeeze you in with a resident who's assisting him."

I drove downtown with my head feeling needled. Sunlight hurt, the pain somewhere behind my eyes. The resident was a blond young man wearing stylish gold-rimmed glasses. He could have been my age. Or five years younger than me. Obviously he was sharp enough to have made it this far in the world of medicine, and as he closed the door I began unbuttoning my shirt.

"First," I said, "I'd like you to remove this."

I turned so he could see the lump.

"You don't need to have that removed. It's a benign cyst."

"I'd like it removed anyway," I said. "Just to be on the safe side."

He shook his head. "It's not cancerous. I promise you, this is nothing to worry about."

"I think it's getting redder."

"If you've been touching it recently, it might appear redder."

"I think it would just be better to be rid of it ..."

"Why don't you wait until you can speak to Dr. Fisk about it?

At your next appointment? If he thinks you should have it removed, you can do so then."

"Fine." I buttoned my shirt.

"There was something else?"

"I've been having trouble sleeping," I said. "Last night, I didn't sleep at all."

"And when did you start having trouble sleeping?"

When had it started? I had to think.

"Well, I had the same problem two months ago, and I guess that was the first time. My wife and I had planned a trip to India. We had our tickets to go, everything was set. I'd never had a problem with planes before but suddenly I felt a fear of flying. It was so strange. I just kept thinking about it, and I couldn't get to sleep ..."

I paused. It wasn't just the flight, was it? He should have more background information.

I said, "You see, I've written a book —"

But I couldn't go on. I started crying! Sobbing, really, as soon as I released that tidbit of information.

The resident pushed his glasses up his nose. Did not speak. Looked at the wall rather than at me. This was embarrassing. Two men — youngish men — in a small room, one crying. But I kept going. He waited for me to get a hold of myself, returning his gaze when I had finally stopped. It took a while.

"Sorry," I said. "Sorry." I wiped my eyes. "This past week it came back. The insomnia. Worse than before. I've only slept a few hours."

He wrote me a prescription for sleeping pills and I departed, grateful.

DESPERATE MEASURES

BACK IN THE GUEST bedroom, I discovered that *The Loggers* no longer held my attention. Maybe the loggers weren't bawdy or quarrelsome enough. The pills had helped for a few nights but I kept waking, kept going back to my problems.

In the day, I had taken a shift at the library's headquarters to help in the computer department. I had no specialized knowledge of computers; the department manager only wanted my voice. Recently the library had acquired a telephone notification system to contact patrons automatically if they had a requested book waiting for them or an item overdue. The department manager asked a female staff member to record the happy holds message but wanted a stern man's voice for the overdue message. That made sense, but three or four men worked in her department — little reason to call me in. "Why don't you just record the message?" I asked the computer department males. "Or you?" But they shook their heads. No way. They wouldn't say why, but I suspected a grade-schoolish shyness about the sound of their own voices. Library staff didn't even receive the messages: I too might have found it disconcerting to pick up the phone to hear myself scolding me for my tardiness. But if only strangers heard? I didn't mind.

Why, if the notification system was brand new, did the hardware seem so low-tech and outdated? It looked as if the department had imported computer equipment from 1982. I sat in a quiet room with metal cabinets holding the library's electronic data and put on a pair of giant headphones with a foam mike attached, watching the screen before me. "Hello. This is the Fraser Valley Regional Library. Someone at this household has items overdue from the _____ branch of the library ..." A graph of pixelated blocks rose and fell. The department manager played the message for me. I sounded nervous. "It's fine," she said. What about the nose breathing? "I can remove all that," she said. "It's a neat little program."

Many people worked for the library system: I knew almost none of them, and left headquarters without having spoken to anyone, beyond a few pleasantries. Should anyone ask about the novel, my standard response was that all proceeded as planned, that I had the galleys, that the book was due to be published in the spring. Back in the apartment, I paced.

I booted up my computer, connected to the net, and used my new search techniques to get more results. I stumbled on a website about Hinduism in the media; the authors claimed to represent thousands of Hindus, and posted complaints about the casual mention of "holy cows" by CNN reporters and insensitive speeches by the likes of Pat Robertson. Misuse of the word "om" angered another contributor, who suggested Hindus copyright the term as a way to protect it from irreligious use. I had used that word perhaps fifty times in the novel and, as with many other elements, used it in a liberal, loosey-goosey speculative kind of way. But what really irked the site's managers was the cover of an

Aerosmith CD featuring what they considered an offensive image: a god dancing among cobras. The artist had drawn a head on the figure that differentiated it from any Hindu deity but the website operators didn't believe this went far enough. To them the figure clearly represented Lord Krishna, and they urged all Hindus to complain to Sony and threaten a boycott. The word repeatedly used for such transgressions was "defamation."

I felt sick. My heart beat faster. Defamation ...? How many ways might these people consider my novel defamatory? In it:

- a Hindu society was strictly governed by caste
- new organs in the body influenced the behaviour of people, and these were called chakras
- the sum of negative influences over people's lives was called dharma

The fictional society had arisen over time, and my premise was that technological changes had co-opted religious concepts to justify themselves. It was meant as a criticism of the embrace of technology, not of Hinduism or any religion. But what did my reasoning matter? Terms I'd used were sensitive, if not sacred, to people like those website authors, and the casualness with which westerners used Hindu ideas upset them. Would my ideas be regarded as casual or insensitive? I had also cast the gods of the Hindu pantheon as giant, mechanical automatons, ruling the land to their own benefit.

By morning I had crafted an urgent e-mail to my editor.

"This is a heck of a time to be having this kind of misgiving, I realize, but ..."

I followed with a ten-point overview of the biggest and most problematic liberties I had taken with the source material and how they might be perceived and received.

My editor had so far defied all of my negative preconceptions of editors. Responding to queries, Michael had always been kind, supportive, astute. I had e-mailed him a few hours prior to our decision not to go to India, asking if he thought it would be a big deal if I didn't provide an author photo taken in India. "I don't think it's a big deal," he had replied, and I'd felt greatly relieved. Now, I paced in the living room. At 6:00 a.m., when he might conceivably be starting work in New York, I could really begin waiting.

The e-mail program made its sound. I saw the subject line of his reply: *Kindly Cool It.*

If your splendid novel was not evidence that you are a writer, surely your e-mail message is: only a writer can be this crazy. I cannot promise you that some fanatic will not come forward and criticize your view of India and Hinduism. No one can promise you that. But it is so abundantly clear that you LOVE India and things Indian that it is hard to imagine anyone — even someone prodigiously and perversely obtuse — thinking of you as an attacker or mocker or in any way hostile to the subject. Believe me, Jan, there is nothing of the guidebook in your novel. You've written a story, nothing more or less — and that is a wonderful thing to have done. And that the setting is India of the distant future — and of a poetic, bizarre, fantastic future to boot — seems to me to make absolutely all your jitters beside the point by several light-years. Jan, please get over this unreasonable and unhealthy fear. Take a deep breath. Take a cold shower. Do ten laps around the gym. Think om.

I had expected him to address each of the ten points.

Michelle woke to find me waiting for her. I explained my discoveries, my realization, my e-mail to Michael, his reply.

"He doesn't get it," I said. "I'm going to send him another e-mail. Or phone him. Maybe the book can be delayed ..."

She took a second look at me. "You can't do that," she said. "I'm not saying this is exactly the same, but there have been times at work when I've gone to my boss over some issue. And then I've gone back to her for more input. She's a supportive person, but finally she had to tell me, there comes a point when it's too much. You have to get over your concerns. You have to have confidence in your own decisions."

This was new. Michelle siding with my editor? With *anyone*, over me? So lacking in precedent was her response that I did wonder, momentarily, if I overreacted and should cool it, kindly or otherwise.

"Don't e-mail him again today," she said. "Don't do anything today, except relax, like he said. You do seem wound up."

When she left for work, I e-mailed my agent. He too replied with assurances that I needn't worry, prepublication jitters were normal, and my book didn't malign anybody or their belief system. He added, "You shouldn't dread a little controversy."

That weekend Michelle left town for a friend's wedding. I tried to relax. I drove into Vancouver to see the restored print of *The Wizard of Oz* playing in theatres, which I had long wanted to do, but the images of emerald and gold flashed before my eyes, meaningless. Afterward, at a restaurant, my friend Stuart commented on my unease and listened to my worries. "People don't get upset about books," Stuart said. "Visual stuff, images and movies, that bothers people. But something in print? They won't even notice."

It was like the night of the bonfire. Back at home, alone, unable to sleep, I got out of bed to pace. I reread my editor's reassurances, and I thought of Stuart's comments, and I knew there was truth in what they told me. I could and did make a list of reasons why I needn't worry. But, as when I had gone out that night and thrown buckets of water and chunks of ice onto the bonfire, nothing made a difference. It was bigger than me. There was just too much material there. The blaze kept burning. I could not stop thinking about it. I could not stop fretting. Maybe nobody who read the novel would be offended. Who *read* it. Would they actually read it, though? Had those website-complainers listened to the Aerosmith CD before passing judgement on the cover? I didn't think so. It existed, and so it angered them.

I went to my file-folder box and dug out something I'd been happy to bury months earlier: my contract with Harcourt Brace. It had galled me at the time, seventeen pages of clauses and schedules, of which a small fraction delineated the financial relationship between the publisher and me. The bulk of it seemed meant to protect the publisher from me. And my novel. *Indemnify.* I checked the dictionary for that word, as I had when I first came upon it, and found again that it meant I should shield Harcourt from any problem arising out of my book: if any financial burden arose out of publication, that burden would be shifted onto me. Oh, and I could imagine the kinds of financial problems that might beset a target as big and inviting as a multinational corporation like Harcourt Brace. I could just see it.

Michelle was still away the next day, and her father suggested we go out for dinner, just Dave and I, a rare opportunity for me and my father-in-law to catch up. I didn't feel hungry when the time came. We went to a restaurant downtown and sat at a small table. The place was hot and crowded. I knew I couldn't put off my news.

"Dave," I said, "I hope you and El will take steps to hide your money."

He looked at me. "Excuse me?"

"It's the book. I hadn't expected this, and I'm sorry. You don't know how sorry I am. Maybe you know somebody who can help you with a hidden bank account — I don't know, I'm just giving you this advice. Please. I'm not sure how long it will take before it happens —"

"Before what happens?"

"My book. I believe Harcourt will be sued by various parties because of it. Unfortunately I signed a contract that will transfer every claim to me, to Michelle and me. We'll be bankrupted quickly. But after that, people will seek damages from everyone associated with us, family, friends, everyone. There's nothing to stop them. Is there anyone you trust enough to sign over your property to? Some third party, to hold it for you? I'm no expert; you should talk to someone who knows about these things. You should talk to someone who can hide your assets."

He opened his mouth to reply, but our steaks arrived. The plates were so big the rims went over the edge of the table.

"You really think you're going to get *sued* over the book?" he said.

"Yes. America is a litigious country. Americans. Very litigious. And it won't just be Americans. It's going to get ugly, over the coming months. Even when there is no financial incentive to do so, they'll keep coming after me, to punish me. I would tell you more, but I think it's probably better the less you know."

I stared at my plate.

Why had I ordered steak? I didn't really like steak. I had ordered it because it was the special and that's what Dave had ordered, and I couldn't focus on the menu items to choose anything else. When I was twelve, I had ordered steak at a restaurant for the first time, on a rare family vacation, because I had reached the conclusion that had Conan the Barbarian been presented with the same menu, steak would have been his most likely selection. Reading the Robert E. Howard series, I had learned that Cimmeria, Conan's birthplace, was roughly located in the region of Denmark, and this was the lone inkling of national pride I had felt as a youth, Conan's roots and mine extending to the same place, and, because Conan and I had so much in common, I had felt almost obliged to request a seared piece of flesh for sustenance. But now? I did not feel hungry. Not at all. I tried. Tried to focus on the act of cutting the meat into pieces and putting each piece in my mouth. Like this was any normal dinner. Two people, enjoying their huge steaks. I saw Dave wipe his brow. It was hot in here. Heat coming off other people in the restaurant, heat coming off the steak in front of me. Was it actually getting bigger? I could feel the heat of each piece in my throat, going down, adding to a heat inside me, making me flush. My steak didn't seem to be getting any smaller despite how much I sawed at it and choked down individual segments. Actual beads of sweat appeared on Dave's brow. Poor Dave. He took out his handkerchief and patted his forehead.

"I've scared you," I said. "I'm sorry."

"No, no, Jan, it's all right."

"I don't know if I'm going to be able to finish this."

"Me neither."

We abandoned the restaurant. I "treated" my father-in-law — if a person could think of eating dinner while being introduced to the notion of his penury as a treat. It had all the pleasure of a last meal.

When Michelle returned home from the wedding, I tried to listen to her recount the highlights: "— and they wore forest green robes on the way to the church, because it was raining, and we all walked behind them, following them into the church. The ceremony was lovely, and my reading went fine. How was your weekend?"

"We should buy this condo from your parents," I blurted.

"What? *Why?*"

"I believe it's a good idea."

"For the past five years, you've wanted nothing more than to move away from here. You've always said you'd *never* buy a home in the Fraser Valley. All of a sudden, you want to buy the condo from my parents?"

"It's a good idea. To protect them. We can separate them from us. There'll be no connection between us. If people go after the condo because we live here, it will not lead back to your mom and dad. They'll have the money from the sale, they'll be safer, they'll be better able to protect themselves."

She went into the bedroom to unpack her suitcase.

I followed her, pacing in the small space not occupied by the bed. I explained the problem and the imminent danger to the happiness and well-being of everyone we knew. It was an awful predicament spanning financial, legal and international realms — all centred on the novel's publication — but I had given it much consideration and could explain my fears quite convincingly. Michelle, who at first had looked confused, soon appeared scared, too.

"Isn't there somebody you can talk to about this? Someone you can get advice from?"

Yes, there was. I had already thought of him, although I doubted anything he did could effect a positive outcome. Still, I must try.

I endured another night without sleep. As soon as business hours began the next morning, I placed a call. "I need to make an appointment for today. Yes, today. It is urgent."

Our lawyer, Ken Fetherling, had been a lot of help navigating my brothers and me through a nettlesome patch of the probate of our father's estate years before, and I had emerged from the experience with my opinion of lawyers improved by his example. He was not venal, self-centred or litigious. During that time he'd done much to put our minds at ease, and things had turned out all right, as he had seemed to know they would from the outset. Of all the people I had dealt with during that process, he came out looking the best. And the luck of it was, we had chosen him almost at random, my brother Erik remembering his name from a notarized document in my father's papers.

The office building had become familiar to me. It was in an area of town that had declined in prestige, an older area with nice older homes with bars on the windows, where a young man on the sidewalk might peer into your parked car, even though you stood nearby. The waiting room of the law offices could easily connote bad feelings, bad times. You almost walked into the receptionist's desk when you entered, and the magazine selection was sure to make the wait feel longer than it actually was. The chairs were leather and wood. A wall just past the desk held an enormous array of gleaming, chrome-plated stamping devices, which at one point I had hoped to see in operation. Today I perched on my chair. "Keep your nose clean," our lawyer had said to me when we had finished with the estate. I had thought it an odd comment, perhaps one he had made mistakenly, by reflex. Maybe I had the demeanour of a defendant, and the conclusion of our business had reminded him of successful conclusions to court cases, perhaps a case in which the defendant was in fact guilty. Maybe it was just his way of saying that he hoped not to see me again, in professional circumstances. How much easier this would be if I were preparing to tell him that I had been charged with drunk driving. If only I were a drunk driver! How I envied drunk drivers.

Today, as usual, Fetherling came downstairs and invited me into the conference room, where law books filled one wall in a tall, uniform block. Fetherling sat across from me with his yellow pad. He was trim, bright-eyed, and seemed to need to remind himself to smile at intervals. We had picked him by chance but might have chosen him deliberately anyway, as he went to the same church as Michelle and her family, apparently a "C-and-E" type like me (Christmas and Easter appearances only), and we began greeting each other at these events with a manly handshake. Maybe he attended church more often and I just wasn't around to see it. One December, I had made some would-be humorous complaint about the approaching chore of going to the Christmas service. "Oh no," he had said. "When I think of all the wonderful memories I have through the years of those services, of seeing my children in pageants, it's something I treasure."

I would have gladly sung carols right now. Anything. I would have sung carols and been arrested for drunk driving on the way home, with pleasure. I would have performed a liturgical dance.

"So what brings you here today?" he said. "What's so urgent?"

I told him. I told him that I had had a book accepted for publication.

"That's wonderful! A *novel*? You should be very proud of yourself. I understand it's nearly impossible to get a book published these days. And Harcourt Brace is a very respectable company."

I sighed. Why couldn't I have just kept my nose clean? And what a terrible way to besmirch it.

"Yes, well, the thing is, I would like you to help me please stop it from being published."

He looked at me. He blinked.

I explained the whole thing: the premise of the novel, my blunder into blasphemy, the inevitable reaction. I felt as if I spoke at a rate perhaps twenty percent faster than my norm. He wrote some notes in his pad. Eventually he stopped writing.

"I understand," I said, "that this may not be an area of law in which you have experience, but I thought that at least you might refer me to someone who does, or maybe you could get the ball rolling while we look for someone else. Maybe an American lawyer is appropriate, someone in New York, I'm not sure, someone, someone familiar with publishing, someone anyway who would be able to help me, help me get out of my contract, stop the book ..."

He waited for me to stop talking. "Look," he said, "I think you're worrying about something that you don't need to worry about. Harcourt Brace is a big corporation, with their own lawyers. Do you think they would publish something that could get them in any kind of trouble? They wouldn't! Their lawyers wouldn't *let* them, and they have much more experience with this kind of thing than you."

"I doubt they thought of this."

"You haven't mentioned it to them?"

"My editor. He's the only person I speak to there."

He sat back in his chair. "I really think you're overestimating the way people will react," he said. "I remember a movie. There was this movie. And people complained because they thought it was a blasphemous idea. The movie was called *Oh, God!*, and in this movie God comes down to Earth, and he smokes cigars and uses foul language. And people objected. They found it upsetting that God should act this way, swearing, and played by George Burns. And I heard all this about how offensive the movie was, but do you know what? I enjoyed that movie. I didn't find George Burns offensive. No! The whole thing was blown out of proportion."

Oh, God, I thought.

The anecdote had veered away from its intended comfort value, it seemed. The upshot was that our lawyer did not think I should be worried. He had stopped writing on his pad. In fact, he drew a line under his few notes, and resumed praising my accomplishment.

"All right then," he summarized. "I won't accept payment for our meeting today. Instead, I expect you to give me one signed copy of your novel when it's published. Okay? See? I'm writing it down here, one autographed copy of novel owing. A deal?"

He smiled and we stood and I limply shook his hand. I couldn't meet his gaze. These were the same gestures and words with which we had concluded meetings during my experience with the estate, but I felt different. Completely different. Hollowed. My last, desperate chance. It had not provided the glimmer of hope I craved. I left the office and felt as if the lawyer now stroked his beard with a puzzled expression, watching me go.

Maybe I could do one thing to lessen the coming storm. A preamble. An apology at the outset of the novel to state that I had not intended offence or harm. Maybe that would limit the bad feelings and backlash. When I returned to the apartment, I put this to my editor.

He e-mailed back to say he thought it was a bad idea. It might have the opposite of its intended effect, predisposing readers to find a fault in the novel that wasn't there. It made me sound like I was guilty of something!

On a purely practical, technical level, it may not be possible anyway to add an element to your book at this stage of its production. Hesitantly, I offer one possibility: If you have a short disclaiming statement (say, a short paragraph) about religions that you'd like to have at the front of the book, we might put that in place of your dedication. If you're set on this — and I suspect you are — then send me AS SOON AS POSSIBLE the state-ment you have in mind, and I'll talk with the managing editor and the editor-in-chief and see what can be done.

I nodded at the screen. I had my task.

I started drafting a perambulatory statement. Making it short was not possible. I rewrote. Rewriting it was all I did for the afternoon. By the time Michelle got home, I could no longer work on the note; the most I could manage was to pace the apart-ment. Poor Michelle! The misery I would cause her and her family and my family and friends ... I blurted to her the events of my day, that it had all come to nothing. She urged me to relax, but my distress passed into her, too. What terrible, terrible luck, for her to have met me. I took my sleeping pills that evening, but again found myself lying awake in bed. I got up and walked through the apartment, into the office. I sat on the guest bed.

I sat in my chair and booted up the computer. I checked the defamation website yet again. What if they could tell? Could people *trace* visitors to a website? Figure out their identity? Would that draw the attention of these angry, righteous people?

I got off that page quickly and disconnected from the net.

There was paper on the desk full of scribbled possibilities, but I couldn't work on the preamble any more. Couldn't look at it. I couldn't go on pretending that anything would make a difference to what I knew would happen. *The Loggers* and the hand-held electronic poker were of no use; I didn't even pick them up. My mind was too busy going through permutations of disastrous outcomes. Once the offended persons had ruined Michelle and me, they would go after my brother Erik and his wife, who would be left destitute. Their children would be taken from them because they could no longer provide for them. My niece and nephew would be taken away from their parents. Their family would be ruined. I was breathing faster with the realization of it.

And *Writer's Digest*.

Somehow, until now, I had forgotten about my piece in *The Guide to Literary Agents*, which would be published next year by Writer's Digest Books, with a huge print run and distribution. That piece reprinted my query letter to my agent and included a synopsis of the novel. People would see the synopsis. Many, many people would see it, object to it for the same reasons and call for the guide to be removed from bookshelves, and if the company relented, if they pulled a hundred thousand copies out of stores and destroyed them, the company would want compensation and would probably seek damages from Harcourt because I had no contract with *Writer's Digest*, and Harcourt would seek compensation from me, and the dispute would get national coverage, international.

How could I get out of this? I tried to think. What was left to do? Could we run away? Start new lives somewhere? But I found no viable solutions. Every scenario led to ruin. The disastrous impact spread wider: I envisioned more and greater consequences.

My novel would be known in India. That was inevitable. *Known, protested, hated.* And groups like the one operating that web page would decry the book. But they wouldn't satisfy themselves with mere complaint: they would try to punish Harcourt for having published it. Harcourt was a big corporation, but could they fend off thousands of legal attacks from a huge country? No. Harcourt would transfer damages to me and I would quickly be ruined, but that wouldn't satisfy the angry population of India, because indignant critics would inflame most of the population. After my bankruptcy, after that, my friends and family. My friends and family could be sued because they hadn't done anything *to stop me* from writing the book. Yes ... It didn't matter if the claim was wild: the publisher, my family, friends, everyone who knew me, they would be susceptible to countless lawsuits, and ruined by them, just attempting to fend them off. This still made for a relatively small target. In a sea of spiralling lawsuits the dispute would grow to pit the country of India against the whole country of Canada. Yes! If somebody could sue my family for not having tried to stop me from writing the book then, logically, people who lived on the same street as me could also be sued, and people who taught me in school, and the university and my profs, of course ... Where would it stop? I tried to think how it might stop, couldn't. There were no limits. The targets wouldn't even be people near me but anyone who lived in Canada. Anyone. It wouldn't matter who, or what they'd done, everybody would be a target. Canadians would lose every case and damages would spiral upward, resulting in a transfer of ownership of everything in Canada, all land, all property, to India. The United States, too. Wasn't my publisher American? Anybody in the United States could be a target, and Americans would sue Canadians because of me. And people close to me would not merely be bankrupted, they would become the focus of the rage of all the Canadians and Americans who'd lost everything in lawsuits. Friends and family would be hunted.

And in India the anger would not diminish. No, Canada or the United States would resist transferring all of their material wealth as the international courts dictated. And then what would happen ...? India would have to use Russia. Yes, only Russia had missiles that could be fired across the Atlantic. India would threaten to fire a nuclear missile at Russia, unless it made a nuclear strike upon North America on India's behalf. And what could Russia do? It had no choice but to give in to the nuclear blackmail. Russia would fire missiles, or, or the United States would make a pre-emptive strike against Russia, one or the other, it didn't matter at that point, because the missiles would be flying back and forth across the world. The end would begin.

Mass destruction and death. That's what I'd done. I knew it. I was the catalyst of all these things. My book.

By morning, it was all so clear. Like watching those sparks leave the bonfire, flying to the forest. I could see the fire now. It began with my book. Every step of the disaster afterward was plain. I tried to imagine ways to stop these events, ways I might halt the process, but solutions didn't exist. There were no solutions. The disaster always found a way around my efforts. My efforts would make things worse. Always worse. Impossible to stop it. Publication. Outrage. Protest. Lawsuits. International lawsuits. Global violence. War. Nuclear war.

Sunshine poured in through windows. It had been fourteen days since the last time I slept through a night, and I had been awake for the past seventy-two hours. But I did not feel sleepy. My eyes felt fully dilated.

I had realized my unique position in the history of the world.

"Oh Jan," Michelle said when she saw me sitting in the living room. "Did you get any sleep?"

"I'm okay."

"I didn't have the best night either. But it gave me time to think of ways for you to relax. I'm writing down a list. I want you to do these things today, okay?"

"Sure."

I was the instrument of the end of the world. I knew that now. My role as such had been performed unwittingly, up to this point, but I couldn't deny it after spending the night looking into the future. The process was horrific and unstoppable. And I recognized it, too, as the will of a force much greater than mere human beings. Events so terrible and cataclysmic could only be explained through religion.

It was no coincidence that the book I'd written that would start the process was titled *Shiva 3000*, Shiva being popularly known as the god of destruction. *Now I am become death, the destroyer of worlds.* Everything fit; this was a time of cosmic import. It was a moment when religions revealed themselves as real, and I saw that, too. Hinduism, Christianity, Islam: I understood that all religions were true, descriptions of one reality, and that certain aspects of individual faiths would rise into prominence, recognizable from one book of writings or another, perhaps, but all part of the same system, the same universal reality. The apocalypse described in Revelation was a prediction of the events about to unfold. Bombs.

Trumpets. Bombs would detonate, people would see through the flesh of their hands. Locusts like horses would descend, with human faces. I had done this, I had set it in motion, I was the instrument of God in his manifestation as Shiva. The world would end. The destroyer had put me in this role.

Michelle handed me the list. "Will you do these things? You can do them before your shift starts, I think."

I looked at the list of relaxing activities.

Number 3: Get a back massage.

"I've already made an appointment for you at Rhiannon's for 12:30."

"Sure."

"You'll do these things? Please?"

I nodded, and drove her to work. As she got out of the car, I told her I loved her, though doing so presented problems: should I say such a thing? Was it immoral to say or do anything that would make her (or anyone else) fond of me, knowing that I was the most wickedly destructive person in the history of humanity? Would positive feelings toward me make her life more difficult, more painful, during the coming firestorm? When I returned to the apartment and sat in the bright light of morning, I continued to wonder, going back and forth in my mind over the ramifications of my actions, trying to decide what was the best thing to do.

I was certain of the terrible end I would bring upon all the world's people, and especially those closest to me, who would suffer the most and the soonest, but I could not determine if actions I took in the interval would aggravate their demise or not. I didn't know. Simply telling your wife you loved her could be an act of unwitting cruelty in my unique circumstance. It pained me to imagine what I might be doing to her in the future. I had to stick with what I did know, which was that I was apocalyptically destructive, and so, evil.

I could not have been selected for this role if I were not evil, and somehow deserving of it. When I reduced my dilemmas to that knowledge, things became clearer. A person of my colossal evil could do just one good thing. Knowing that, I could not turn from it. I could only do it, and be over.

I put on my jacket and crossed the street to Safeway.

On prior trips to the grocery store, it had seemed as if I'd noted hundreds of products suitable for use in disposing of oneself. Michelle and I had both worked at Safeways during the summers while going to university, and because we lived so close, we shopped here almost daily. I knew the aisles well. I knew where to find most items. But somehow today, under the fluorescent lights, I had trouble finding the best product for the job.

All of the shaving equipment came in plastic casing that minimized the edges of the blades. "Don't you sell straight razors any more?" I wanted to ask the pharmacist. But this might cause problems for him or her later. He or she would likely hear of my death, and that might cast a real pall, if he or she remembered helping me find the razor blade. I also worried how my actions might influence people in coming days, because I didn't want to affect the chances of those who would be left behind to experience the apocalypse. Yes, I was damned. This I accepted. But I shouldn't risk dragging other people along with me.

Also, a question about where to find straight razors might be interpreted. The pharmacist might intuit my plans and say something, or even try to stop me. I had to be careful with the cashiers, too, because many of them knew my wife and me personally and might notice a difference in my demeanour and look at my purchases and inform Michelle or do something else to thwart me.

Was somebody watching me?

I looked both ways down the aisle.

Perhaps I'd been standing here too long. I hung the bag of Gillette razors back on its stem. Wouldn't that be unfortunate — if store security grabbed me, thinking I was a shoplifter, and stopped me from completing my task? I quickly walked to another aisle like any other shopper who was not the bringer of the end of the world.

The floors had recently been buffed, making light pool under my feet. The dog food section. A happy Irish setter leapt against a green background. Think! I knew what household products could kill a person; why couldn't I remember one now? That dog looked so happy. Even his ears seemed to be smiling. Puppy Chow would be no help. I feigned interest in the bags. In case someone watched. The manager had an office affixed to the ceiling, didn't he? Maybe he watched from up there, thinking I was a shoplifter.

Think.

I had read about suicide methods. What had I read?

During a particularly boring shift at the library, I had pulled *Final Exit* off the shelf. What did this mildly controversial book actually contain, I had wondered? I'd flipped through the pages, thinking perhaps the info would someday come in handy for a story or something. And now I struggled to remember. The Irish setter continued to grin, frozen in mid-leap, as I recalled an early chapter, or maybe the preface. Something about ways a suicide attempt could go wrong — with results worse than life itself. A bullet could take surprising turns inside the head. A car crash was unreliable, dangerous. You could end up on life support and be a burden to your family for decades! The one foolproof suicide method I knew was jumping from the top of a very tall building. We lived on the fourth floor, and I was pretty sure that was not high enough to guarantee anything but pain. Also, I didn't like the idea. It was messy, obviously, but also too shocking a display. Not what I wanted.

I walked back and forth before the dog food. Another thing, an important thing, was that suicide attempts had a high failure rate, and the book had suggested having a backup method. In other words, kill yourself by different means at once, so as to minimize the chances of survival. Two ways, was it? Well, I thought, better to be thorough. Three. Three was my magic number.

Safeway no longer seemed a good source of supplies. Less and less did I like the idea of going through one of the tills. What might that do to the cashier who sold me, say, oven cleaner, then later learned of my demise and connected back the dots? Would she be haunted by the small talk we had made? Wonder if something she said had spurred me on? No good. Not right. I had to do this myself, with no help from Safeway, and I tried to think of what we might have available at home. A knife was easy. That was one method. A plastic bag and string to tie it. Two. And ... what else? Of course! How could I forget? I already had sleeping pills.

Three. *Three.* I left Safeway, relieved to be away from the store and yet have my solution.

In the apartment, I decided there was something I should do. I booted up the computer and connected to the internet.

In coming days, when the disaster began, I knew things would be traced back to me, and intense interest would surround what

I said and did, especially during these final hours. Cracking open my Hotmail account would pose no problem to the FBI agents assigned to learning what it contained, and when they did so, they would find the e-mail I now composed. In it, I wrote of my self-recognition as a prophet, and how I understood why society despised prophets: they threatened the material comforts of people, and this, I had discovered, was exactly my role. My foreknowledge would become public, as someone would surely leak this e-mail to the media, and, as events unfolded exactly the way I had predicted, people would accept my terrible power of vision and the information come upon me. Before the worldwide firestorm began, I urged all people to recognize the universal spirit that I had stumbled upon and identified.

> ... whether or not the earth is touched by a spiritual presence is made mysterious mostly because we are incapable of surviving long enough to really see for ourselves. But what led to my convincing was a simple question: Why is energy? Physicists come up with long and elaborate explanations for the history of the universe, but they won't tackle the question of why energy exists, because it is fundamentally unapproachable ...

I explained my realization of the night before, and wrote on a piece of paper the simple equation that summarized it. This was all a person needed to know to look at the universe: e? The "e" stood for energy, and the question mark for: why does it exist? Why does energy exist? All theories returned to the subject of energy. The big bang was all about a great sudden burst, but if you asked yourself why energy existed in the first place, you would know: it could not be, without something to bring about its existence. There was no cause within energy itself. So something outside of time, the universe and the laws of the universe must exist. Call that thing God. Call it a cosmic force, call it whatever you wanted. The name mattered less than the fact of its existence, and that was what religions struggled to explain. It wasn't that any one religion was more or less correct: all religions were right, because they pointed to the same thing. Yes! The approaching disaster was described in the Christian Book of Revelation, but being the cause of this cataclysm, I also recognized that I was an agent of the universe as destroyer and creator, as Shiva. Different points of belief might find favour with different people or become more tangible to them at a particular time, but it all supported the same central premise, it all worked toward my formulation here in the apartment.

$$e?$$

The simplicity of my formula impressed me, every bit as elegant as $e=mc^2$, yet more profound and consequential to mankind. Maybe $e?$ would be widely distributed among people and become symbolic, a symbol of this new cosmic awareness, as the cross was to others. I hoped some good might come out of these few paragraphs I composed, that after Armageddon maybe my words would remain and perhaps form the basis of whatever society re-emerged. I didn't know if that would happen; I couldn't foresee everything.

I signed off with an appropriate last comment: *amen/om.*

Having sent the e-mail to my Hotmail address, I packed my briefcase: string, a carving knife, a plastic bag and my bottle of sleeping pills. And some library books. Then I headed off for my very last shift.

QUIET IN THE LIBRARY

PATRONS OFTEN SAID they liked our library because of its small size. Here, they could keep an eye on their kids in the children's section while they flipped through a magazine at the far end. This was important to many of the people who came, having moved to a rural community for the benefit of their children. From behind our checkout counter and desk, it was not as easy to see all of these spaces because, over the years, we had acquired things like an internet station and video collection, and the librarian had been unwilling to jettison our paperback racks or any of the book-shelves. I appreciated this and was always willing to drag a spinner full of paperbacks into new configuration with its neighbours, hoping to free up a few more inches of space so our heftier customers too might enjoy the novels of Louis L'Amour without being pinched. It was cluttered. The building was about as long and wide as a mobile home and of comparable building quality. It appended a community centre, a kitchen and a hall that bore the lingering odours of budget wedding receptions and dog obedience lessons. Our door was next to the shared men's room, and on a few grim occasions, Gail and I had been made to know the bowel movements of elderly men. We tried to make sure this door always remained shut. Windows behind our desk and on the opposite wall provided light, but at a height that prevented us from seeing anything other than a spray of pine branches. We couldn't see into the parking lot.

Small talk had never been a talent of mine. I lacked Gail's gift for springing into conversation on some topic or other that somehow engaged the other person and coaxed them into actually replying. Disappointingly, my mind sprang toward stock phrases or an observation that might offend the person across the counter from me. *I don't think babies should have their ears pierced.* Or: *Do you make your own clothing?*

That shift, my co-workers and the patrons would not think I was particularly quiet. My reasons for being quiet were very different today. Singular. Knowing my role in the end of the world, I didn't dare talk any more than was necessary to get through this shift. As with the Safeway cashiers, I didn't want anyone who came into the library to remember anything in particular about what they had said to me, prior to killing myself. I didn't want to put any spin on their experience of the apocalypse. Bad enough that after my death, I would continue reminding people that they had overdue books, thanks to that message I had recorded for the computer department. Would people regard a message on their answering machine as a freakish souvenir of my passage, when my true nature was revealed to the world? I imagined skittish types jumping out of their windows when they came home to hear the voice of me, the destroyer, agent of God as Shiva, in their living room, scolding them for having an overdue book.

I thought about things like this as I smiled and nodded, sliding books across the counter to pleasant Mennonite families. A boy who'd once pressed me for information on the Iditarod, with plans of entering the race himself. And a woman who consulted a notepad to ensure she wasn't checking out a book she'd already read. Another I'd known since junior high, then a smoker, now someone who dressed like the characters depicted on the covers of the Janette Oke novels she read, women who knew both prairie toil and wholesome longings. *Forget about me. All of you. Don't remember our exchange, it's nothing.*

My plan took shape: maybe a half-hour or so before the library closed, I would complain of feeling unwell to Gail and ask if I could leave early. She would let me leave, as she sometimes needed to go home with a migraine herself, and was by nature easygoing. That would give me an extra half-hour on top of the one that driving home usually took, before Michelle would start to wonder why I was late. More than enough time to drive to the location I had thought of, an old logging road my friend Dave and I had discovered while mountain biking, very secluded and surrounded by trees. "This would be a great place to dump a body," I had joked at the time. Now I considered it the perfect place to park a Honda Civic, do what I must do, and ensure that I would be several days dead before some unfortunate hiker happened upon the scene.

Knowing the time of my death almost to the minute imbued the checking-in and checking-out of *The Hungry Little Caterpillar* with a new dimension. It put a different spin on clock watching. I had no doubt that this was my only option, the only certain good thing I could do with what my life had unexpectedly become, but I wondered what awaited me on the other side, after I tilted back the seat of our car and watched its fabric-padded ceiling fade from view. I certainly expected the worst in whatever afterlife followed. How bad would it be? How badly would I be judged for my actions of the past twenty-four hours?

I thought of that e-mail sitting in my Hotmail account.

When I got a break from the desk, I went to the computer, logged in and saw the message sitting there, waiting, unread.

I questioned myself. What did I know of the future, after the apocalypse? What right did I have to try to steer people toward a better civilization afterward? Maybe my message would have the opposite of its intended effect. Maybe people would view me as the devil on earth and do the opposite of what I had suggested. That was the sort of vast irony that could happen in such a cosmic moment. An act meant to be good could turn out very badly. This was a lesson I had actually learned.

Still.

Maybe I had been *meant* to send that e-mail, exactly as written. Every word. I couldn't discount the possibility that after having arrived at my celestial knowledge, everything I did was exceedingly meaningful and fated to be. But I wasn't certain. I didn't dare delete the e-mail. This was another dilemma, another hard situation. I decided that the most honest option was to state my lack of certainty, in a second e-mail. Cast some of my own self-doubt onto the first e-mail. Maybe this would cause a rift between two rival camps that arose in the new civilization, each side disputing the validity of the other's sacred e-mail, and a horrible conflict would arise out of that, too. I didn't know! I couldn't know some things, and that too was torturous. As a safeguard, I sent the second e-mail to my Yahoo account. Maybe both e-mails would be found, maybe one, maybe neither. God could decide that.

So went my coffee break.

I could minimize my interaction with people during the shift, focusing during lulls on tasks that allowed me to avoid people. After dusk, our page came in for his shift. He was the son of one of our favourite families, also of Mennonite descent, and often started shelving books without us having exchanged a word of greeting. Nothing unusual in that.

Time passed. Those high windows showed darkness and a few branches, and the occasional flickering glow of an unseen lamp somewhere in the parking lot. Gail went home for her dinner break. She tacked her coffee break onto lunch, to maximize the time she had at home. "Don't work too hard," she would say, departing. Or: "Have fun." Or: "See you at seven." This was troubling, trying to reconcile my last few hours alive with the mundaneness of what was just another Tuesday evening at the library for everyone else. I wouldn't see anyone again. There was no such thing as fun any more. Work? I felt terrible for what I had done to everyone, but especially people like Gail. My mouth dried, looking at the minute hand of the clock. Soon I would have to do it. Be done with myself. I feared the coming moment, feeling the press of that old knife on my wrist, and I feared what dying would be like. My fear surprised me. I knew I must kill myself, but this didn't make me any braver. Too bad. More punishment, I supposed. Nothing should be easy for me now.

I walked to one end of the library, stopped for no reason in particular, lingered, returned to the desk. Our page may not have noticed. He was a teenager. He had his duties and they absorbed him. Meanwhile, I drifted. Short aisles, tall aisles. Here, many years ago, a copy of H. P. Lovecraft's *The Shadow Out of Time* had found a place in the collection. I remembered the shelf. The approximate location. I walked back to our work area and turned off the radio, which we left tuned to CBC. It just didn't seem right to listen to the theme music of *As It Happens*, when you were preparing to die.

"Excuse me?"

Someone waited at the counter.

I walked over, unsure how long I had stood staring at nothing, thinking.

Less than an hour and a half until the shift was over. I wondered if, when I got to my place in the forest, I would have difficulty swallowing so many pills. Worse, what if I vomited them up? The best strategy, I decided, was to start taking them before the shift ended, a few at first, more toward the end, and drain the container when I had everything else prepared. In the washroom I took my first. Fifteen minutes later, I went to take another, but realized this might look suspicious if I continued after Gail returned, so I put on my fleece jacket, poured a goodly number of pills into my pocket and brought a Styrofoam cup full of water back to the desk with me. I took a few more pills.

My voice was a little slurred when I was forced to answer a patron's question. I wanded the barcodes of books with decreasing accuracy.

"Uh, I think you missed one," a kindergarten teacher said.

I corrected the omission for her benefit. I could see just how sloppy my work was. A hippie couple looked at me with disbelief as I pretended to check out their book on how to make a straw-bale house. Hopefully they would not comment on my manner to anyone but each other, assuming I was merely stoned.

The checkout computer had access to nothing but the library catalogue. I looked at the work desk, with its newer monitor and terminal.

What if my e-mails had already been discovered?

It was very likely that the FBI monitored e-mail communication for certain keywords and dangerous concepts. That being so, wasn't it likely that someone working for an American agency had already seen my message?

Yes. They had *definitely* seen my e-mails. And those authorities had had enough time to verify the details of what I'd written and contact law enforcement here in Canada. Probably they had already begun a drastic emergency action, in response to my electronic disclosure.

I continued to move about the library and pause here and there, randomly. Our page stopped what he was doing. It was unusual for me to wear a jacket while working.

"You all right?"

I nodded.

Few patrons remained in the branch. The only sounds were keyboard clicks from the public internet station and the occasional rattle of that lamp outside, shaken by the wind. A slow night.

Or.

Or maybe not a slow night. Maybe the police were out there already. The RCMP, responding to the tip off from authorities in the States, had already come to the library. Police cars were parked outside. A special squad. To deal with a unique situation. They could not let me live, of course. Outside, marksmen quietly prepared. They didn't want to alert me to their presence, so they waited for people to leave the library on their own. But as patrons left the building, the police hurried them away and made sure that nobody else went inside. Bullets would soon fly. That was why so few people were in here. That was why.

The phone rang. "Yes?"

"Jan?" It was Gail. "I'm still at home. Sorry! We had friends from out of town drop by unexpectedly and we've just been visiting and visiting. Would it be okay if I didn't come back right away? Can you hold down the fort by yourself?"

"Sure," I said. "Okay, Gail."

"Great, thanks a lot."

I put the phone back in its cradle. Now I knew for sure. They had asked Gail not to come back in, too. Maybe she stood in the parking lot. Using a special phone the police had given her. They didn't want her to go back inside, either.

They could not let me live. I understood. I had earlier realized how violent the reaction would be if I continued to live after delivering my prophecy. That was part of why I had preferred to take my own life. Now I would step out those doors into the sights of rifles. It would be a gruesome, shocking end, sure to draw attention to my role.

I rubbed my forehead.

It was all over. Forty minutes or so remained until the library was scheduled to close, but what did that matter? I no longer made an effort to hide my pill taking. I sat at the desk, throwing them back.

Another patron left, giving me a strange look. Good. Go. Be safe. Why did I still make a show of working, anyway? When I had a half-hour to live? Why go through this charade any longer? I stood and lurched around the library.

Our page had stopped what he was doing again to stare at me.

"Are you sure you're okay?" he said.

"Go home," I told him.

"What?" He checked his watch. "It's only 7:30."

134

"Just do what I'm telling you and leave the building. Now."

He put down his books and walked toward the door, looking at me with extreme puzzlement as he went by, holding his hands upturned as if to say, *what gives?*

"Tell your parents you love them," I said.

He was gone.

Just one person remained in the library.

She sat a few feet away and had watched this exchange between the page and me.

She was a nurse, upgrading her skills; I knew because on several occasions I had helped her at the internet station to access a database of nursing journals, with articles she needed to study. We had gotten along well. She sat in front of the internet terminal now and watched me very closely, her eyes wide.

"D-do you want me to leave, too?" she asked.

I nodded.

Her purse was on the floor and without looking at it — keeping her eyes on me — she leaned down to grab it. Then she stood quickly and rushed past me, out the door.

I went back to the work area and sat in the chair.

The library was dead quiet. Still. I was the only person here. No reason for any delay. *The police must know that.* Didn't they realize I was alone in here? I looked around at everything, trying to soak it all in for the last time. I had spent so much time in here. I had walked around here with my mother once. All these books. The same children's section was right in front of me. A boy might choose a book on being a veterinarian, or a fireman, or a backhoe operator. I could have taken out any of those books. It seemed like this was a place that might influence a lot of decisions. Picking which books you read. There was a lot of chance represented in the way they appeared on shelves, what would come up before you on a spinner full of books. Things could have been different. Somehow, from those days to this moment, it amounted to a path. Why had I reached this moment? Made so many bad choices? If I could go back ... But I could not. I had already followed the path. The end was near.

What were those marksmen and snipers waiting for? Why did I wait, for that matter? There was no reason to wait until eight o'clock. I should just step outside now, get it over with. I looked at the door. Go outside, let them shoot me. Be done with it, be finished, be over. I didn't want to feel those shots, hear the sounds — it would be awful. But if that was the way it must end, so be it. I should let it happen. I didn't want to die, but it must be done.

I sat in the chair. Another problematic decision. Should I initiate my own killing? The shooters outside might be eager to pull their triggers, but it was still killing a person, and wrong, wasn't it? What were the ramifications ...? Maybe it wasn't wrong to kill someone like me? As evil as me? Maybe that made it okay? I shook my head. I didn't know ... Hopefully the marksmen would spare me this decision. Hopefully they would storm the building if I waited just a few more minutes, or should I not wait ...? Trying to decide what to do was torture. Couldn't I be spared the decision, at least?

I watched the door. Heard the doorknob turn. *Finally.*

Finally, the door opened. I inhaled. Swallowed dryly. Tried to keep my head up.

But it was not the sharpshooters. It was ... *Gail?*

"I see you've been run off your feet!" she said cheerily. "Jeez, quiet in here tonight."

I watched her round the path toward the desk. What was *she* doing here? Had the police sent her inside ...?

"Well, that was a really nice surprise, we haven't seen those friends in ages," she said, setting down her purse. "Thanks again for holding down the fort."

Standing behind the counter, she stopped to look at me. I stared back at her.

"Where's Alex?" she said.

I didn't answer.

"Jan?"

"Are they out there?"

"Is who out there?"

I didn't like to say it differently. "Are they waiting for me to go outside? Is that what they want me to do? Is that what I'm supposed to do?"

She cocked her head to look at me. "Jan," she said. "What's the matter?"

"I ..."

"What's the matter?"

I shook my head and covered my face. She hugged me.

"What's the matter? *What's the matter?*"

PART THREE

Character Problems

HEARTY FAKE LAUGHTER

ALMOST A WEEK HAD PASSED since Gail had phoned her husband to come to the library and drive me to the hospital. There I remained, a patient of the ward.

Another day faded, as I again sat in a place where I could maintain my vigil, watching the courtyard and adjoining buildings. And at last, after so many glimpses and hints of nearness, the federal agents appeared.

First I heard them. Their words stayed beneath the level of my understanding but I could hear voices, low voices, outside. I sat up straighter. Following the conversation to its source, I spotted one outline, a second. They moved against the dropping sunset, but once I had seen them, their presence was undeniable. The two men wore coveralls. They no longer bothered with discretion, and they passed back and forth on the other side of the window with an occasional comment. At last. Finally.

So why did they wait? Why not just storm inside? Maybe they didn't have permission to make their move until after sunset — I remembered how the RCMP officer had seemed impatient with the night nurse, waiting for her okay to proceed. If these two came inside to take me now, in the early evening, it would make chaos here and a lot of work for the nurses to restore order.

No point in resisting: I knew my arrest would come sometime and, as with other consequences of my terrible cosmic blunder, I could do nothing but accept this development. Trying to avoid the agents would be futile. If not now, later. The most I could hope to achieve was minimizing the distress of people around me. I didn't want to be the cause of turmoil.

I got up from the couch and walked through the emergency exit.

"Here I am," I announced, stepping outside.

The two men in coveralls paused. "Uh ... here you are, what?"

"I'm the person you're after."

They looked at one another with raised eyebrows then went back to an old air-exchange unit.

I stood nearby, available. They dragged the piece of scrap equipment over to a truck and got ropes out of the cab and heaved the unit onto the bed and strapped it in place. They got into the truck and started it up. As I watched the vehicle drive away, I began to think maybe they wouldn't arrest me.

I returned to the exit. But from this side, the latch of the handle wouldn't depress. I rapped at the window to catch somebody's attention. The door opened.

"Thanks, Dorothy," I said.

"You're welcome."

She shuffled back to her jigsaw puzzle.

No need to mention to anybody why I'd stepped out. If no staff members noticed my latest encounter, or if they didn't ask me about it directly, the incident didn't count. False sightings of federal agents would hurt my chances for discharge. I returned nonchalantly to my seat on the couch. The thing to remember was that just because I didn't notice the nurses observing me didn't mean that they were not observing me.

The next morning Bernard hurried about, more garrulous than usual as he watered plants, greeted nurses by name and indulged Ruth, but he broke away from her monologue to cheerily resume his ward chores. He was showered, shaved, neatly dressed. All signs seemed to indicate that he was in love with life. This was preparation, I suspected, for his morning talk with the psychiatrist. Afterward I watched Bernard emerge from the office, his chest fallen. "The doctor thinks I need to stay here a few more days," he reported forlornly. He walked toward the lounge, dragging his foot. It had again become anchor-like. I shared his disappointment more than he knew. His efforts, though, reminded me where I needed to place my own.

"I'm feeling pretty good," I told Dr. Brophy when my turn came to sit down across from him and his tie. "I've been doing normal activities, as you suggested. Talking to people. Vacuuming. Michelle and I sometimes play Scrabble in the evenings to pass the time."

"And how has that gone?"

"She always beats me. My worst scores ever."

"You're at a disadvantage."

"I'm not one of these people who learns a bunch of tiny words that nobody ever really uses except to rid themselves of Scrabble tiles," I said.

"Do, re, mi, fa, so."

"Exactly. I think they should be against the rules. If you don't use a word in everyday conversation, you shouldn't be able to put it down for a triple word score."

"And how has your sleep been?"

"Pretty good. Thanks for changing my medications. Last night I had a dream. My aunt — actually she's my great-aunt — asked me who Karl Malone was. I tried explaining who he was and, as I did, realized I didn't know myself."

He smiled. "Sometimes a dream indicates something we're worrying about but not expressing during the day. Other times it's just a little joke from God, something He gives us to smile about."

I cocked my head and nodded. I had truly never thought of dreams in this way before. I had only mentioned mine because I couldn't remember the last time I'd had a cohesive dream and was glad to find this one lacked riffs from my waking nightmares. That was the angle I hoped he'd note.

"And what about your concerns about the book?"

"They're not as bad," I said. "I'm still a little concerned, yes. There's a story in the news. You probably heard about it — in Surrey, fights at a Sikh temple." The dispute was between Sikh moderates, who wanted chairs and tables to be allowed in the temple, and traditionalists, who did not. Debate had led to violence, which had led to big coverage in the media. "I saw the picture on the cover of *The Province* yesterday, and I said to myself, I am not going to look at that story. I don't want to get into that."

Generally I had avoided the news, as I didn't want to stumble upon anything that might confirm my fears, but the Sikh temple story did not, in truth, concern me. My feelings centred on Hindu issues and reactions, and a fistfight in the parking lot of a Sikh temple meant little more to me than one in a Catholic schoolyard. But I expected that staff here would make no distinctions between Sikhism and Hinduism. Or rather, I thought that they thought I wouldn't split hairs when it came to nearby religious violence in an Indo-Canadian community, and so I fulfilled what I presumed to be their expectations. Anyway, it seemed a good bone to throw to the nurses and the psychiatrist. I didn't want to appear to be recovering too quickly. People might think I was faking it.

Another story making headlines in *The Province* interested me much more. For now, though, I measured what I shared with the doctor. A day or two before, Michelle had asked me something noteworthy. "What do you think of Dr. Brophy?" she had said quietly.

"I think he really wants to help me!"

"I'm sure he does," she said. She looked at her hands; she picked bits of lint off her sleeve.

Was my answer wrong? I did believe it. Most of the time. Some of the time. While a student, I had given the Thomas Harris novels close readings, trying to learn what made the plots so compelling. The unintended message of *Silence of the Lambs* was that a psychiatrist could be a serial killer. I recognized that as a fictional device, and a stretch at that, but the non-murderous psychologist in the book, Chilton, comes off worse than the criminals he minds. Now, plots of my own making grew and fell on a daily basis, and often I rotated and spun Dr. Brophy, trying to understand if and how he fit into them. I knew better than to say this aloud, but Michelle's question made me wonder if she knew something.

I concluded the meeting feeling that I had done well. Out of the office, I glanced at *The Province* for any more mention of the story that did intrigue me, about bargaining talks between the government and the Hospital Employees Union.

Before I could settle into the lounge for another day of sitting, staring and keeping my theories to myself, I saw the social worker wheel in a video machine and TV. That morning we would see another feature, this one without any tenacious, kind-hearted lions ascending to jungle royalty.

"She's really good," said a staff member as she plugged in the VCR. "Her name is Doreen Madsen and I think anyone can benefit from her lectures. I've seen her in person."

I helped drag chairs over from the eating area, and other patients were summoned. Where was Angela, my phobic chum and safe conversationalist? Maybe she was avoiding the crowd, but much time had passed since the last time I had seen her, and it occurred to me that she might have been discharged. Lucky woman! But I regretted not having said goodbye to her.

The video started. Onscreen, an audience applauded the appearance of Doreen Madsen. She was a large woman wearing a comfortable dress, all the better to move back and forth across the stage and gesticulate. Doreen, we learned, had risen from tragedy. Her husband had left her, her father had died in a boating accident, her Shih Tzu had bitten her — it had been a terrible week. But despite all of this, or perhaps because of it, Doreen Madsen was about happiness: making your own happiness. This is what she had done, and this was the idea that she was apparently paid to tell large audiences. In her floral-print muumuu and chunky necklaces, she introduced the idea that happiness took effort, that it wasn't applied to your life from an unseen, external source, like a dollop of mayonnaise to a ham sandwich. You had to work at happiness. Cultivate it. Feeling blue? Unable to stop feeling blue? Perhaps you were more to blame than you knew. Doreen offered simple exercises to prod us back toward feeling good. She told us a catchphrase I would hear several times: "Fake it till you make it." *Fake it till you make it.* If you wanted to stop feeling miserable, the theory went, you should begin by pretending to be happy, by imitating the physical mannerisms that indicate happiness. It could work! If you tried! She goaded her audience into making that grimace of ecstasy known as a smile — even if the resultant face did not accurately represent your inner state, even if you actually felt the melancholy of a confessional poet — put a smile on your face so big you could feel its endpoints biting into your eyes. A good laugh was also useful. Come on, laugh! A real belly laugh. She placed her hands on her belly and chortled. A laugh from deep within! Ha ha ha! Come on now! Her studio audience did as instructed, laughing at one another in a disturbing display of fabricated hilarity that suggested an obscure group of cultists who sought to bring down the roof with laughter before they drank their tainted Kool-Aid. I joined them. When instructed by Doreen, I, too, smiled maniacally. Maybe a rubber chicken would help! Why not?! She hung one around her neck, a necklace of pale simulated chicken flesh. I placed my hands on my stomach and laughed. I couldn't help but notice that in the ward audience, I alone followed Doreen's directives. Ruth seemed uninterested. Bernard watched with his arms crossed. I could appreciate the reluctance of my fellow patients: the last TV personality whom I'd taken directions from was Mr. Dressup. Responding — vocally — to a video of a self-help guru? A few weeks ago I would have considered this an indication of a deep character flaw. But I dutifully laughed or stood up or leered at my neighbour — whatever Doreen commanded! — not because I thought her methods would yield results, but because of the location of the TV. We faced the nurses' station. I wanted to show my willingness to receive suggestions from helping professionals and do the work necessary to improve my mental state. I would fake it until I made it. At least, I would fake it until I made it out of the ward.

CONTRACT TALKS between the hospital union and the Ministry of Health had bogged down. The topic crossed from newspaper pages and TV reports to the mouths of staff around me. If one union stopped working, others would refuse to cross picket lines, making for a chaotic situation in which the hospital could offer essential services only, and the more the nurses around me spoke of staffing woes, bed shortages and the potential impact on patients, the higher my spirits rose.

When Michelle came to visit the next afternoon, I had a surprise for her. I sat waiting, wearing my jacket, with my packed bag at my feet.

"I've been discharged!" I told her.

"Discharged?" she said.

It was true. There I had sat in the lounge, looking my sanest, when one of the nurses gave me the good news. "The staff is getting ready for a strike!" I said happily. "They want to get the number of people in the ward down to a minimum, and I think Dr. Brophy was ready to discharge me, anyway. I'm coming home."

"But — okay, well wait. Sit down for just a second. I want to talk to the nurse."

I didn't want to sit. I feared someone might reconsider if I lingered too long. After Michelle had spoken to the nurse and confirmed what I told her, we headed for the double doors. "Goodbye, everyone!" I called to the nurses behind the glass windows. "Thanks for all your hard work!"

The male nurse shook my hand. "Happy to be going home?" he said.

"Uhhhh ..." I rolled my eyes and looked upward, tilting back my head, throwing aside my arms. This was not among the gestures Doreen Madsen had taught us but it conveyed the immense relief I felt.

Michelle wanted to be pleased. We got in the car, and I sensed she was glad for my boosted cheer, but also she seemed distracted, uncertain. Maybe the abruptness of my discharge was to blame, the surprise of it. She was a woman who liked to see things follow their intended steps, and the lack of a final summary meeting with all the people involved in my stay bothered her. "I just don't want you to be short-changed in your care because they're worrying about a strike by HEU."

I brushed this aside. "We'll still have that meeting. And I'll see the psychiatrist at his office. The only difference is whether I'm staying at home or staying in the ward. And there's no reason for me to continue staying in the ward. There's no benefit to me being there. This makes perfect sense."

It wasn't the first time I'd been back to the condo since my admission, but the return had never before given me such pleasure. There was the garage door, just as I remembered! The elevator! How I loved the elevator. Inside the apartment, I took a moment to absorb the sheer beauty of the carpets and the walls and furniture. Then I put down my bag and retrieved the phone number for my editor in New York.

"What are you doing?" Michelle said.

"Phoning Michael."

"Do you have to do that right away?"

"I want to catch him before he's finished for the day."

"I mean, do you have to do it today? You just got out of the hospital ..."

"He's been made to wait too long."

Michelle had in fact contacted Michael while I was in the ward to tell him to go ahead with a brief preamble he had composed for the book and not wait for mine. She had not shared any information about my fears or my discoveries on the web. About me, she'd only said that I was "sick." Well I had big news for him. Huge.

I collected myself and dialled. The first thing Michael said when he got on the phone was, "That's a long time to be sick." He sounded a bit sulky — perfectly understandable, given the length of time since he'd heard from me — but his tone changed immediately when I recounted events since then.

"Oh my God!" he said. "I had no idea! I'll have a look at that website and get back to you. In the meantime, just take care of yourself. No book is worth that kind of anguish, Jan."

I hung up feeling satisfied. I was out of the ward and had told my editor the problem. Someone who could actually make a difference to the production of the book now knew my secret. I didn't feel like I alone held the key to the end of the world. Maybe it wasn't the end of the world — I knew my thinking was skewed, and a possibility existed (slight possibility) that all I had done was write a novel. Whatever the case, I felt improved, and the conversation felt like an extension of my happy, happy discharge. Now I could really celebrate: I could shower, and stand on a wet surface where no unusual feet had been. I phoned my brother Erik to tell him that he need not worry any more, I was out of the hospital and pretty much recovered. Michelle and I watched *Holiday Inn* with Bing Crosby and Fred Astaire, and I thought the movie had an interesting plot structure, considering its vintage.

Home gradually lost its power to comfort. Night came, escorted by familiar problems. I remembered what I feared. The bonfire was always more apparent after the sun set; the fire became the only thing I could see. I didn't mention it to Michelle, though. I was out of hospital! I was recovered! But how was I going to protect her again ...? How had I thought I would protect her?

We went to bed. A married couple going to bed — it was normal. Except that this felt like a test. In this room I had experienced insomnia many times, but now we knew it for a sign of my mental problems. Sleeplessness had preceded craziness, had aggravated it, maybe caused it entirely. We were aware. We said goodnight as if this were any other night, but neither of us could shake that knowledge.

I lay.

I lay, shifting and turning, trying to get comfortable. Comfort was not coming. What had happened to our mattress? It used to be so welcoming. When we had come home from our honeymoon in Turkey, lying down had felt like a reunion with a beloved friend. Now the mattress was full of sawdust and balled newspaper. It was a bale of peat moss.

Bad enough that I couldn't sleep: Michelle, too, kept readjusting her body position and breathing in a way that suggested alertness. We kept each other awake with the sounds of being awake. We lay.

"Can't sleep?" she said.

"Not yet."

"What are you thinking about?"

"Things," I said.

"Like what?"

I hated this line of questioning. I preferred not to tell her. But when asked, I also felt that I couldn't lie. My head seethed with thoughts of good and evil, sin and non-sin. "There are three parts of a person," Dr. Brophy had told me, "soul, spirit, and body." I needed to improve all three, I believed. I'd be off to a bad start, lying to my wife.

"You," I said.

"What about me?"

"How sorry I am."

"Jan, you're thinking about it again, aren't you?"

"Just that I'm sorry to have dragged you and your family into this whole terrible situation," I blurted.

She exhaled. If she suspected I might answer in a manner that she disliked, why ask in the first place? In the ward we'd had this conversation several times, and it had nowhere to go but in circles, or a spiral, a widening spiral of fear and frustration.

"You're no better, are you? You're still having the same thoughts."

"Not all the time."

"When don't you have them?"

I didn't answer. If I didn't know the right answer, it would be a lie to say the wrong one. No more lying. Except for on the bed.

"All that time in the hospital," Michelle said, "you were just strategizing how to get out."

"I was not strategizing!" Everything I had professed while in the ward about my inner state was what I started to feel, or what I worked toward feeling, what I would soon — no doubt very soon — think and not think. It wasn't *strategizing*. No, that made my efforts sound so ... deliberate. Calculating.

"Why haven't you fallen asleep then? It's almost midnight. If you're feeling like yourself again, why can't you sleep?"

"I just keep going through the same thoughts, over and over and over ..."

She sighed. "What did the psychiatrist suggest you do when that happened?"

"Pray," I said.

"*Pray?*"

"It's supposed to relax the mind. A relaxed mental state."

"Pray," she said. "All right then. Pray. Fine, let's pray. I've been praying my whole life: no reason you shouldn't start. Should we pray together?"

We recited the prayer every Christian was expected to know, but as I spoke the words, the sense did not enter my head, as mentally I continued with another, quite different plea, the one that I had authored myself and that was my single request to the deity with which I had so recently come into contact: *Please do not destroy the world please do not destroy the world please do not destroy the world ...*

For a long time we recited the prayer. Eventually our voices dwindled. Silence. We waited. Sleep hadn't come upon us, nor did I feel any more relaxed. No, I felt reminded. Of my faults and transgressions, of the slim chances by which the world might survive. I could feel Michelle's tension through the mattress.

She got up. "Come on," she said.

"What?"

"We're not sleeping, this isn't helping. We've got to make you more tired."

She set a pot of milk on the stove to warm and we went into the living room for another lengthy game of Scrabble. BOX. LATE.

RUN. I wasn't hugely fond of Scrabble; circumstances had made it our default entertainment, if "entertainment" was the right word, and, as had been the case since this began, the play was made more laborious by the small, uninspired words I managed to assemble. The tiles didn't branch across the board so much as form a disorderly queue in the centre. It was a mumbled exchange. A list of first words for a student of English as a second language.

Ninety minutes later we gave up on the game and made another attempt at sleep. We repeated our earlier conversation. I couldn't deny that my thoughts constantly hovered around the same points, the same as before. I couldn't shake myself from the cycle.

"You're not better," Michelle said, and I could hear the tightness in her throat, the changes made to her voice by building tears. "I don't know what to do, I don't know what to do."

"You don't have to do anything," I said.

"We can't go on like this."

"It'll be okay."

"How? How will it be okay?"

I didn't have an answer.

"You came out of the ward too early —"

I said, "I am not going back."

"Listen to me for a minute —"

"There's no way I'm going back. I hated it in there. You have no idea."

"I know you did, but — where are you going?!"

"I just have to use the washroom."

She sat up in bed. I could see the outline of her, upright. "Leave the door open," she said.

"I'm just going to the washroom, all right? Nothing else."

"Leave the door open!"

This was more humiliation than I had expected for my first night back in the apartment: not as bad as nights in the ward, but still. Had I not conveyed to her well enough the discomfort and unease I had felt in that place? Didn't she understand? Didn't she know that the ward itself contributed to my distressed view of the world, that that *place* did more to reinforce my theories of conspiracy than to dismiss them? She usually understood me so well. Usually she at least tried to swing her point of view around temporarily to better understand mine. Obviously she didn't know that I no longer had any intention of doing myself in: that was why she wanted me to leave the door open between bedroom and bathroom. There was much she didn't understand, apparently. I washed my hands and walked back into the bedroom.

"You have to believe me," I said. "I have no intention of killing myself any more!"

"I want to believe that. But I never would have thought you would try in the first place. I never would have guessed. This is all new to me. I'm confused." She wept as she spoke. "I just think you need more time —"

"I'm not going back there."

"Jan." She closed her eyes and opened them. "It's not just you I'm worried about. I'm sorry, but it's me, too. If you become delusional again — I don't know if you're going to do anything to me."

I was dumbfounded. That I had not expected to hear. Hurt her? It was crazy! I would never ... It was just such a crazy, crazy idea. How could she think ...

"Will you let me take you back to the hospital? Please?"

I dropped my head.

We returned to the hospital a few hours later. Michelle had phoned first, and whomever she spoke to had asked her to wait until 6:00 a.m., presumably when the night shift ended and when the slumber of other patients wouldn't be disturbed. Outside the big orange doors, a night nurse came out to readmit me. Couldn't she just grab my file and cross out "Discharged" at the end? No. I submitted to the process. This nurse seemed blasé. No mention of the novelty of my case this time. She chewed gum unapologetically as she asked questions, filling out a form on her clipboard.

"Do you use drugs?"

"No."

"Do you cry more easily than usual?"

"Yes."

"Have you noticed changes in your sleep patterns?"

"Yes."

"What would you say if I said to you, 'People in glass houses shouldn't throw stones'?"

"I would say, that's a clichéd expression, which like all clichéd expressions is sometimes handy in everyday conversation, but in writing and in formal communications, should be avoided."

She paused for a beat, then made a mark on her sheet. No, I did not hear voices. The name of the country in which we lived was Canada. The season was fall. Or winter. Yes, I did think I was ill. Yes.

She put her signature on the bottom of the sheet and stuck the clipboard under her arm as she stood. "You're depressed."

"I am?"

"You haven't heard that in your diagnosis before?"

"No."

"Whaddayaknow," she said, opening the big orange doors.

I said goodbye to Michelle. She had to go to work in a few hours and I felt awful about that, about everything. I told her to go home and try to get some sleep. Then I re-entered the ward.

I didn't know about depressed but I certainly felt miserable. The lights were turned low, just bright enough for people to find their way to the station, and the station itself was bright. The lounge and eating area were deserted, the patients sleeping in their rooms. It was almost December. Given the length of my first stay, and because I had not improved during it, I knew I would be in the ward through the holidays and into the New Year. After I had hung my jacket and put my stuff in my new room, I walked back out to the main area and saw the next shift arriving in the station, the nurses chatting amongst themselves with that excitement I vaguely remembered from shift changes. Among the arriving workers was the male nurse who, the day before, had so warmly wished me luck upon discharge, and seeing me now, he broke from conversation, confusion plain on his face. I lifted my arm so he could see the new plastic bracelet around my wrist. He emerged from the station.

"Jan? What are you doing back here? What happened?"

"I couldn't sleep," I said. "Just couldn't get to sleep. Still."

"I'm sorry to hear that."

"This must be the shortest discharge in the history of the ward," I said.

"Oh no," he said, with a chuckle. "Believe me, Jan, it's not the shortest." Then he paused, tilted his head and hurried away before I could prompt him for an example of a shorter one.

THE MEETING HAD ALREADY been scheduled, as a discussion of my discharge, but now, with circumstances changed overnight, the gathering lacked any breath of joy, accomplishment, satisfaction. The hospital's social worker, a nurse from the unit, Dr. Brophy, Michelle and I all sat around a table. Michelle had called my physician but he hadn't shown up. The meeting took place in the same room where my fellow patients and I had screened *The Lion King*. The blinds were half-open today but I was too full of self-pity to concern myself with who might be watching. Bad enough to be the subject of a meeting, even worse for the subject to have become my failure to get a grip.

Michelle described the previous night, the frustration and failure, for the benefit of those assembled.

"Perhaps," said the psychiatrist, "you tried too hard to succeed."

"Tried too hard?" Michelle said. "Maybe Jan was discharged too soon."

Silence. It was strange to sit in a room where people felt permitted to speak so candidly about you.

"I think we need to consider Jan's behaviour once he got home," the psychiatrist continued. "You say the first thing he did was phone his editor. Obviously that caused him stress and rekindled his fears and worries about the book." He opened his hands. "Maybe the real question is, why did Jan do that? Why did he phone his editor?"

"I phoned him because you said I should let the truth be my guide," I said.

He lifted an eyebrow but didn't respond. Actually I would have phoned Michael no matter what, but that bit of advice from the psychiatrist had weighed heavily on my thoughts, and making the call fit into the breadth of its demands, as I interpreted them.

Michelle mentioned the idea raised by the gum-chewing night nurse: that perhaps I suffered from depression. This was pertinent. Nobody before her had so confidently ventured a diagnosis. My treatment had begun with mild intervention, based on the possibility that I only suffered from a severe case of stress-related lack of sleep. When the insomnia had continued, I had been treated accordingly, but with no improvement to my paranoid state. The drugs had changed, but still I couldn't shake the delusions. Perhaps I was bipolar. That fit with some of my characteristics. Later my physician had told me he thought I was becoming schizophrenic. But depression? Dr. Brophy did not think I was depressed and said so.

"With all due respect," Michelle replied, her voice shaky, "but I think we would benefit from a second opinion."

Nobody else said anything.

"Fine," said Brophy. "Fine."

He appeared diminished. I believed that my wife was the one person whose opinion I could trust, that whatever view she took in such discussions was also mine. Often I envisioned my psychiatrist as the RCMP's partner on the unit who used Bernard to sniff out information from patients that law enforcement here and abroad might find interesting. But at this moment, I felt badly for him. His judgement questioned in front of his peers. Had his shoulders fallen? Maybe. This was my failure. I didn't like to be anybody's source of embarrassment. I was the one who had performed badly, not him.

The meeting ended, and I tried to absorb the fact of my re-admission. Michelle spoke to one of the nurses and passed along the miserable conclusion that they "hadn't had enough time to observe me" during my first stay. I interpreted that to mean fewer passes out of the ward and more time under their scrutiny now. Worse, when I had been shown to my new room, the sheets on the other bed were tousled and personal items sat on the bedside table. No privacy this time. No niceties. No nothing, except for a long stay as a regular patient.

In the afternoon, as I lay in bed not regaining the sleep I had missed the night before, a nurse came and said, "Jan, you have a visitor."

"She's back already?"

But it wasn't Michelle. It was her father, who wanted to show his support with a brief stop. But here I was in my pyjamas, and I could view him only as the father of the woman whose life I had ruined. Realizing it, I broke down.

I pulled myself together in the semi-privacy of my new room and saw the young man with whom I'd be sharing it. His legs were like jointed chopsticks, and his body seemed to taper as the eye travelled up from his waist. His tall back was hunched, perhaps due to the weight of his head and glasses. He was pale, with thinning blond hair, and previously I had noticed him mumbling as he knocked around, long legs carrying him on meaningless trips about the ward.

A gentleman in a suit had pulled up a chair beside him, and I took the opportunity to eavesdrop.

"Now Rodney," said the older man. "Later you may notice that the nurses have changed your sheets. There'll be a rubber sheet underneath your regular ones. Don't let this bother you — sometimes the nurses have to do things like this for their own reasons."

Rodney seemed to take no offence. I, on the other hand, wondered what was planned for me in the middle of the night so traumatic that seeing it would cause my roomie to shit himself.

The day wore on. I hadn't filled out the chit yesterday to say which meal option I preferred, and so I had to choke down soft broccoli and a battered piece of utility-grade pork. Additionally, a can of something called Boost sat on my tray. I read the label, then leaned over to tap Rodney on the shoulder. "This must be yours," I said.

"No, Jan," said a nurse, overhearing. "That's your Boost."

Meal supplement? Give me a break, I wasn't that thin. Now that it had become a subject of discussion, however, I felt obliged to pop open the top and take a swig. It made a poor after-dinner drink. Processed vanilla, I think that was the flavour. I gazed at the mix of familiar and new faces at the tables, the patients who would be my companions again, forever. I felt as if I'd drunk the milk from a bowl of sugary cereal.

AFTER DINNER MICHELLE came to visit, as was her habit.

"Jan, there's someone who'd like to speak to you. Do you feel up for that? His name is Dr. Whitman."

He would provide the second opinion Michelle had asked for at the meeting. Her request had already been granted.

I was surprised to be greeted in the office by that same dark-haired gentleman who had braced Rodney for his change in sheets. Whitman was the other psychiatrist assigned to the unit; I had seen him a few times on the ward but never considered his role. He was well dressed and dignified in manner, saying after we sat down that he was pleased to meet me, and he did seem genuinely intrigued by my situation and my delusions. As I had several times before, I explained the end of the world I had foolishly brought about.

He put the tip of his pen to his lips and gazed upward for a moment. "I don't know," he said. "It seems unlikely that any country would get so upset over a book as to launch a nuclear missile. When they haven't done so over territorial disputes? Or control of resources?"

I shrugged lamely. I could see that from some perspectives my dire predictions might — just might — appear implausible. Later I would learn that staff had advised Michelle against both contradicting and reinforcing my delusions, not knowing how I might respond. But here in the office, Dr. Whitman gently argued against a few key planks of my doomsday scenario. He was the first person to bring up the unfortunate reaction to *The Satanic Verses*, a parallel to my situation that I had been expecting someone to make for some time. "That was Muslims who were so upset, of course, not Hindus."

"And I'm no Salman Rushdie," I said.

He chuckled.

The encounter put me in mind of meeting with a university prof, the psychiatrist talking about my problems as a prof might try to help a student having a difficult time with a paper — prompting, but not in a way that removed the challenge of the problem or its intended lesson. I almost expected to shake hands with him upon the conclusion of our discussion. Out of the office, I told Michelle that I found the man easy to talk to, that I felt more comfortable with him than I did with Dr. Brophy.

Dr. Whitman agreed with that night nurse and thought an anti-depressant was a recommendable addition to my drug regimen. I began to take it that evening.

MAYBE THE ANTI-DEPRESSANT was to blame, but to me it seemed I was afflicted by the problem of truth.

I went to bed that night anticipating whatever shocking encounter would cause Rodney to void his bowels. I woke sometime after 1:00 a.m.

"Mmmf ... Noooh!"

Expecting my executioner, I sat up in bed. But it was only Rodney, struggling on the other side of the room.

"... merfummff ... heehh ...?"

What was the matter with this guy? Why so noisy, Rodney? In addition to the turning and shifting, he mumbled nonsense in his sleep. Could a rubber sheet be that uncomfortable? I got up and walked to the nurses' station to beg for a sedative strong enough to shield me from my roommate's nocturnal emissions. Staff could drag me away in a coma when they came to get me: that would be my preference, anyway.

But I found myself still in the ward the next morning. Michelle seemed encouraged by the second opinion. "When you are eventually discharged," she told me, "we can choose who you see, and maybe it will be Dr. Whitman? I mean, you did say you felt more comfortable with him, didn't you?" Yes. But while in the ward, I would continue to see Dr. Brophy. I felt uneasy going into my next meeting with him.

"Let the truth," he said, "be your guide."

This was not the first time he had given me this piece of advice. Or did he say, Let the truth be your guardian? Or your lantern? I can't remember the exact thing he suggested the truth should be to me, but whatever the wording, he clearly thought that truthfulness was essential to my recovery. He repeated this today with emphasis. Was he looking at me differently, too? I felt his gaze more keenly. On prior occasions I had certainly agreed with the concept: I was accustomed with the value of honesty, but on the other hand, I hadn't wanted to be so honest that I had to stay one day longer in the ward than necessary.

Today, though. Why say it today? What did he *really* mean? *Let the truth be your guide. Guardian. Lantern.* It didn't occur to me that perhaps he, like my wife, sensed that I strategized to get out of the ward and was not altogether forthcoming in our discussions, and that, given my readmission, perhaps now was the time to start opening up and talking about things that troubled me. No, instead I deciphered his comment. *Dr. Brophy didn't believe me.*

That was it. If he emphasized the truth, then he must think I lied. Lied about what, though? He didn't think that the novel had precipitated my crisis, maybe. He actually, privately, thought that I had done something much worse, some physical crime, and that I had tried to kill myself because I couldn't live with my guilty conscience. When I first met him, hadn't he expressed his disbelief that the novel's publication should so badly distress me? No, he didn't believe that was it. Couldn't believe it. So what did he think I had done? Poisoned someone? Tried to purchase a houseboy from Thailand? What? He wanted to pry a confession from me that he could hand over to his contacts in the RCMP. I would have to use extra caution in what I chose to say to him. Whenever I felt suspect, I remembered that accusative stare of the woman cop. *What had the police already been told?*

Then again.

After our meeting, returned to the lounge, I wondered. Maybe the psychiatrist was onto something. Truth. Did my problems stem from the fact that I was not truthful? My greatest aspiration to this point in my life had been to make a career of creating not-true stories: I had embraced falsity. And it had embraced me, maybe. Seeped into me, into my fibre, my personality. What I did on the page presumably had an effect on who I was and what I did in daily life, how I interacted with other human beings, didn't it? Falsehood was what I had taken to heart. That was me to the core, and no wonder I found myself here in this place, and damned.

I would stop that, right now, right here. Why not? I had to remake myself from the inside out.

I would not say anything untruthful ever again. If put in a situation where social convention demanded that I tell a white lie, or say something more harmful than good to another human being, I would reply with silence, and no verbal promptings or funny looks would break my pious hush. That afternoon, I ate my lunch very quietly. Though I received a bruised piece of fish with oily potato slices rather than the chicken salad sandwich I had requested, I voiced no complaint. To be truthful, it was easier to be very, very quiet.

The next step was to be truthful in my thoughts. If you should be truthful in what you said and did, then by extension you should be truthful inside your head. I would never again think anything deceitful. Did I want to share my table with Ruth? Or did I, in truth, want to eat alone? I shouldn't pretend with a welcoming smile that I was pleased to see her pulling out the chair next to me if in truth I wanted nothing more than a table to myself. It was easier to remove myself to a new table than decide what exactly was truthful.

It couldn't stop there, though. A lie was a lie. If I thought, "The bushes in the courtyard look nice today," I had to stop and also think: Did I really mean that? Or did I actually think they looked like good hiding places? Was I just thinking that to cover up, yet again, my true feelings and worries, as I had to Michelle and Dr. Brophy? What did I think? Was I telling myself a lie, or a truth? The answer was, I turned away from the windows.

Impossible to turn away from everything, though. On the TV, a newscaster spoke. "A high school car wash that was supposed to raise funds for this year's graduating class turned to tragedy today." I couldn't listen without many thoughts springing to mind, and each asked for expulsion, due to a high content of falsity. I sat farther away and pretended I couldn't hear. But I could hear, couldn't I? Wasn't that the truth?

"I'm going to lie down for a while," I said to the nurse, walking out of the lounge.

My steps wavered. My thoughts ran so thoroughly with the falsehood of my thoughts that I had difficulty walking. I tried not to look at things, for fear of the falsity the sights might spark in me. When I reached my room, I got onto my bed and sat, cross-legged. I had to find things that were safe to think. That was the solution.

What did I know? Without doubt? The Earth is round. No, I didn't actually know that. Maybe if I had walked the globe with a compass and sextant. *I am a person*, then. No, that wasn't established. God is real. Yes, God is real. That is safe. God is real, God is real, God is real. I rested my head in my hands and thought only that, over and over. I stared at the weave of the bedspread without letting it interfere. I could feel other thoughts, external thoughts, possibly false thoughts, *lies*, all swarming, hovering, waiting, at the periphery of the one thing that I knew for certain, and I had to focus on the one true thought and exclude, without thinking about them, all of the many, many lies that my mind craved to circulate. God is real God is real God is real —

Don't think that! Don't think what you were about to think!

That was the background sensation, a twitch of mental muscle, and if I kept it up at the border of my consciousness, nothing false could penetrate. Don't let anything else intrude. There was nothing else. Hold nothing but truth. Just one thought: God is real, is real, is real.

The words lost meaning. I don't know how long I repeated the silent mantra before this happened. It was like thinking about a single word for too long and finding that it lost its sense. But that was okay. If I lost track of what the phrase stood for, that didn't make it less truthful. The single thought that I allowed in my head was right, and so I was no vessel of lies. My surroundings faded as I focused on the one idea, little more than a pattern, a jumble of mental signals, words reduced to pulses in the brain, and no actual concepts infringing upon them. It was a swirl, and I felt I could let go, keep letting go until I lost the ability to make meaningful notions.

I was at a crossroads. I knew I could give myself over to going nuts. Just lose it. Think nothing. Wear a tatty robe and slippers for the rest of my life. Traipse down hallways. Mumble to myself, but never again really talk. I felt I could depart from all but this one stream of unspoken syllables and never re-enter what had been my world. This seemed the only way to be as truthful as I needed to be. Truthfulness could only be maintained if a person gave up higher thought, and I could do that. It felt possible to give myself over forever. I could do it. *Do it.*

But I disliked the feeling. Distrusted it, too ... Did I want to lose everything but that one thought? Being devoid of falsity made me feel no stronger. I didn't feel any more resilient, sitting on my hospital bed, nor did I feel improved as a person. It took an effort to fend off secondary thoughts and emotions, to maintain a mode of perpetual defensiveness, and I felt uneasy pitting myself against naturally occurring notions. And it frightened me, being so close to the haze. The swirl of nothingness offered to my personality scared me. As much as I wanted to be devoid of falsity, I feared losing my mind.

Maybe I could allow some false thoughts.

A few lies. Maybe a few were necessary.

To maintain sanity, maybe a bit of self-deceit was required — permissible. I didn't want to be crazy, really. As much as I wanted to be a non-liar, I discovered that even more, I wanted to function. Maybe I would be damned for not making enough effort in my self-improvement. I didn't know.

I lifted my head. I sat on the bed. In my room. I felt relieved, with my decision. I let myself look at the walls and think whatever I would think, seeing what was around me.

The other bed. Bathroom. My spiral-bound notepad. I sat for a time.

Hinges squeaked. I looked at the wardrobe. Its door had opened, slightly. I stared at it. Silence.

"You can come out," I said.

No reply.

"I know you're in there," I said to whoever was inside the wardrobe. "You can come out. I won't put up a fight. You can come out …"

VERY TRICKI WOO

WHILE IN THE WARD, I received three pieces of mail.

The first was a card from the regional head of the library, the boss of Gail and me. The front featured watery, pastel irises. *"Don't worry about your job!"* was the message inside. In truth, it hadn't occurred to me before that perhaps I should worry about my job. But I appreciated the thought. I wondered what kind of conversations were going on among people who knew me.

The second was a care package from Gail, whom I hadn't seen since she had discovered me in my severely unbalanced state of mind. It was a box of products from the store on her farm, and I was as impressed by the packaging — a professionally printed box of the sort that could withstand international mailing — as the contents themselves. She too had enclosed a supportive note.

The third was a large and heavy box from my brother Erik and his wife. I had told Michelle that I wanted *no* visitors during my stay in the ward. This was partly due to my lingering delusions — I didn't want to jeopardize anyone who came into contact with me — but I also felt embarrassed. I didn't want anyone I cared about to see me in here. I often wore pyjamas. Due to my issues with the shower, my hair looked even worse than normal, greasy and unkempt. What good would visiting me do anybody? To see me like this? No thanks. Erik had planned to drive down here from Prince George, a full day's drive that included much time in the winding, twisty, prepare-to-meet-God Fraser Canyon, and I had used the payphone to call him and urge him to stay home. "Why bother?" I had asked him. "We can talk just as easily on the phone. You'd come down here and have nothing to do." He relented. But he doubtless wished to do something for me during my stay, and so came the weighty box.

I tore off the packing tape and unfolded the lid. Underneath balled newspaper, books. Many books.

The ward's small collection sat above the games shelf. "Listen to me," Ruth said one day, seizing one of the books and the nearest nurse. "These are valuable, I assure you, true collector's items. I don't know the precise value but I can tell you it is very high and I urge you to please, please have a professional appraiser take a look at these books and make sure that you insure them against loss or damage." Gilt-edged pages and leather-like binding did lend the books a certain dignity, but they contained versions of famous novels condensed by the staff of *Reader's Digest*, and I suspected that Ruth had neglected the laws of supply and demand in her evaluation. Anyway, they weren't for me. But with the long hours I spent in the ward, I craved something to read.

Michelle had told me that she'd looked in my room for books to bring me. "I wanted something to give you comfort," she had said, "but I looked and looked, and couldn't find anything."

I could think of no comforting books in my collection, either. I didn't hang on to childhood reads. The few sentimental favourites remained because they represented a time in my life when I could really get into a novel about a group of travelling vampire hunters. This was not such a time. Fiction by the likes of William S. Burroughs and Thomas Pynchon, which I had enjoyed more recently, was also disqualified. Hallucinatory prose is no fun if you yourself are hallucinating. The constant running through the years represented by my fiction collection was conflict well rendered, whether accomplished by battle-axes in adolescent material or divorce proceedings in a short story collection by John Updike. But who could guess what dramatized conflict might stir in someone who sat alone and delusional in a psych unit? I could see Michelle's challenge. The non-fiction material in which I had recently immersed myself was no better: tomes about mythology, religious beliefs, India. Most of my reference works connected in one way or another to the novel. If I myself had been given the task of picking a palatable book, I might have whittled the contenders down to *The Loggers*, and sadly, the bawdy, brawling men of the Pacific Northwest had negative associations for me now.

This delivery from Erik was good: reading material with no connection to my life, selected by my brother, a physicist with a rational mind who knew the particulars of my paranoid delusions and could make selections appropriately, and whose taste resembled mine, apart from genre stuff.

P. G. Wodehouse was the author of the first book I took from the box. My notions of his work were vague and informed primarily by illustrations on the covers I'd seen at the library. It surprised me that Erik was a fan, but I could certainly use some dry British wit, and this novel seemed just the right kind of entertainment for the setting.

I tried to read about Jeeves, but I couldn't get it. Every time, after I had read a page or two, I realized I didn't know who any of the characters were. Jeeves? Wooster? Who? The plot was incomprehensible. Erik might as well have sent me one of his physics texts.

Faced with an absence of comforting books in my collection, Michelle looked to hers. I confessed my difficulty with Jeeves and Wooster, and she brought a simpler book that she'd enjoyed many times through the years: *James Herriot's Dog Stories*. I was determined to comprehend this one. I could see that the text was largish and the stories were short, so I knew the material could not be difficult.

I also knew by their reputation that the books dealt with the humorous, life-affirming travails of a veterinarian from Yorkshire, presumably the friendly looking fellow who in the cover photograph stood with two dogs against a backdrop of rolling green hills. The first story in the collection, "Tricki Woo," was told in the first person. I struggled to determine that the narrator was the veterinarian.

The text presented greater difficulties. The description of the setting quickly became clouded in mention of cocktail biscuits and excellent sherry. Where was he, again ...?

Within three pages I had lost track of the names. Who was the pet owner and who was the Pekingese? Tricki Woo? Mrs. Pumphrey? Neither held their designation. It didn't help that the character invented stories for her dog in which he wrote letters to a magazine and verbally passed judgement on a new summerhouse. I restarted from the beginning, thinking I was just too distracted, but once more the story offered surprising reversals, with results that would have given William S. Burroughs hives. Was it the woman who suffered from flop-bottom? *Whose* anal glands needed to be evacuated by the vet?

I closed the book, hoping that the staff hadn't noticed how many times I had flipped back to the first page. I put the bookmark ahead of the spot I'd actually reached and smiled, as if my heart had just been warmed by the thought of a woman curled up to snooze in the lap of her small dog.

But thinking: I am crazy. This was proof, as bad as when I had sat on the bed feeling my mind slip. Or my brain had been so poorly rewired that I could no longer comprehend even gentle animal stories.

Whichever the case, I should keep it a secret.

THE BELIEVERS

IT WAS DECEMBER NOW. Almost a week had passed since my readmission to the unit. Night fell, and the sound of squeaky wheels and drawers being unlatched made my throat muscles move in anticipation. The cart had come noisily out. Time, yet again, for my medicine. Medicines. Loxapine, oxazepam, doxepin, alprazolam, risperidone. As needed, I also took haldoperidol, lorazepam, benztropine. Michelle had told me the names but they meant nothing to me: they hardly qualified as words. They were as manufactured as the pills themselves, and I thought this was why I could never keep them straight. Ox. Pine. Az. Am. That was my prescription. Hal. Rip. Lor. Pick a syllable, fuse it to another and clip the result with the official sound of a *done* or *ine*. Alpamodine. Doxedone. The forged word needed only to suggest science and recovery. Naming drugs was easy for whomever that task fell to; keeping the names straight was impossible for me, sitting at the far end of the process, consuming. But not what I worried about. I took pills. Accepted them, as part of this place, part of my place, being here. They were what I did.

After the cart was locked up and wheeled from view, I didn't go to bed. I declined to follow that part of the routine. I wouldn't. I sat in the lounge — just me, the windows to the courtyard and an exasperated nurse or two. That was my concern: who lurked outside, in the darkened yard. What he would do, when. Frustrated nurses took turns sitting beside me, trying to persuade me to go to bed.

"I saw you had a visitor today," said one. She meant Mr. Anderson.

"Yes," I said.

"And did you find his visit a comfort?"

I told her I had.

"I don't think much of him or that church," she continued. "But I think you should go back to your room and remember whatever he told you. That's my advice."

Didn't think much of him or that church? This seemed an unnecessarily candid thing to say, and one difficult to reconcile with the soft-spoken, thoughtful fellow who had earlier come to see me. He was a friend of Michelle's, a retired minister with many positive associations for her, and he had married us.

Years before, when Michelle had taken me to one of the Christmas or Easter pageants and introduced me to him, he had asked, "And what church do you go to, Jan?" I had smiled. It had satisfied me to think he didn't have a clue who I was. I had remembered him very well as the minister who, fourteen years earlier, had spoken at my mother's funeral and who had visited her in hospital just prior to her death. He was a good person, I knew, but I associated him with everything I had discarded around that time. Prayer had not helped my mother one bit.

Until then, I had prayed every night of my life, too: even more when she was ill. I even prayed for a few weeks after she died, until I asked myself, *Why am I doing this?* It was worse than futile. When my mother most needed a reply, none had come. I felt like a fool.

On the day after my admission, Mr. Anderson came to talk to me. I remember coveting Michelle's stability — she would never find herself in a situation like the one I had made, I knew, and that was a function of her personality, which I attributed partly to standardized religious beliefs. I longed to corral my catastrophic personal revelations back into something resembling normal thinking, and I hoped that Christianity would at least downplay my role in the undoing of the universe. That first day had been hazy with drugs, sleep deprivation and delusions, but I do remember him visiting and the first question I asked him: "Do you think redemption is possible for someone who is thoroughly evil?" He probably wondered whether I had bludgeoned the schoolchildren or merely poisoned them. But after a pause: "Yes!"

Later he had gone to our apartment to assist Michelle in following my elaborate instructions for deleting the Hotmail message. I had customized the sounds our computer played, so that whenever it shut down, it repeated a line from the movie *Blade Runner*: "I want more life, fucker!" Previously this had struck me as sheer hilarity, but it seemed less funny when I learned Michelle and her minister friend had rebooted the computer several times and the killer robot repeatedly cursed them.

When Anderson visited me a second time at the ward, he found me more lucid and asked if a Bible was available. There were none in the lounge — a wise decision on somebody's part — but I thought I knew where to find one.

I went to my room and saw Rodney lying on his bed.

"Do you have a Bible I could borrow?"

"Sure."

He produced a square of rich, dark leather with a golden zipper around the side. Unzipping the case revealed a gilt-edged King James Bible, locked in place by a stainless steel mechanism, with a notepad and fancy pens stored in pockets on the other half.

"Nice one," I said.

I took the weighty object back to Mr. Anderson. I appreciate now that picking a Bible verse for comfort is not easy when the intended recipient is hallucinatory and beset by delusions of cosmic grandiosity. Anderson did have something, though, and it did help cool my ideas. He paused a moment before reading. "Now there's a reference here to a book," he said. "Don't worry about that, it's not your book they're talking about."

I could accept this. I copied down the passage before returning the Bible to Rodney.

That evening, both of us lying in bed, Rodney asked what I'd wanted his Bible for.

"Uhh ..." I checked my notes. "Psalm 129."

"Awesome," he said.

I shouldn't have been surprised that someone with so elaborate a Bible might know its contents well enough to recall psalms by number. But Rodney's example was not as encouraging as Michelle's. I knew Rodney was religious because strains of his readings surfaced in what he mumbled in sleep and when he bumped about the ward. Godliness was not a sure defence against madness: most of the time Rodney seemed thoroughly distressed, even tormented, by that breadth of knowledge. He and I seldom spoke. Outside of our room, I avoided him. Not long after lights out, he'd start mumbling in his sleep while I lay there, trying not to attribute any special significance to the cryptic phrases he burbled.

Dr. Brophy was aware of my ambivalence about religious ideas. He had never told me what particular branch of Christianity he preferred, but I suspected that if he was forced to choose between receiving communion from a gay minister or erecting a billboard with a spooky message on his lawn, I knew which he would pick. This made me feel awkward whenever spirituality came up in our conversations. At our next morning meeting, he sat across from me with his penetrating stare.

"Have you been reading the Bible?" he asked.

"No," I said.

"Why not?"

"I don't think I can handle it. I'm worried that I'll see some phrase or other and connect it to my theories of the end of the world."

"Before you open the Bible, you must ask for wisdom," he said, and glanced ceilingward.

"Mm," I said.

I knew how the story ended. If forced to choose between relying on a dose of heavenly wisdom and taking a chance on flipping through Revelation only to find mention of me, I knew which I would pick.

Outside of his office, though, I considered good and evil and how I measured up. I had accepted the possibility that I might not be the destroyer of the world — this was possible — but my thoughts had turned to my life and decisions that shaped it, and even if I wasn't fundamentally wicked, I realized that I had made choices based on self-gratification, the most obvious example being the pursuit of a career as a fiction writer. A desire to help people had never motivated me. No, I had hoped to be seen as gifted, that was what it reduced to, and if my motivation wasn't evil, it was undeniably self-centred. I must incorporate good acts in my life — selfless behaviour — if there was to be any chance of feeling comfortable with my place in the universe. I wanted to make this change immediately, to make an effort.

But what good could I do here? The primary problem was that I didn't want to talk to any other patients. Bernard, Ruth, the woman who walked around as if trying to touch her ear to her shoulder: they were all freaks, weren't they? On the other hand, people in glass houses ...

I watched Rodney. He strode through the ward ceaselessly, muttering to himself as he went on his gangly way, his brow creased and his eyes looking ready to produce tears of remorse. He walked and walked, and I realized he walked like I thought, my mind going over and over a finite number of possibilities, him exploring every possible route through the tables and chairs. I hadn't really spoken to any other patient since Angela's departure.

I stood, predicting his journey, and got in his way.

"Do you want to play ping-pong?" I asked.

"Sure."

His muttering stopped. He helped me clear the table and scare up a pair of paddles.

Ping-pong should probably be declared the official sport of mental patients. The pairing just seems right: something to do with the sound of that taut plastic sphere hitting the table, the back and forth of it, the unexpected angles, not to mention the platypus-bill oddness of the implements with which you were expected to manage the ball's frantic ferrying back and forth. It was an excellent choice for two obsessive minds. I had entered the match thinking I was doing Rodney a favour, and that I would have to go gently with him in his condition, but he quickly established his superiority with the paddle. For my part, watching the ball whiz past me, I found that our setting offered a new field of excuses. *You're lucky I'm taking so much Haldol.* Ping-pong went so well that Rodney and I began exploring the games shelf. We passed over Master Mind and a game premised on the dealings of real estate magnate Donald Trump, others with the corners of their boxes separating and held together by hospital stickers that said "Allergy Warning," in favour of the dented Chinese checkers board, the rules of which Rodney needed to teach me, and shuffle-board, all excellent contests for him. "I'm going to ask the psychiatrist to reduce my meds," I would threaten, "then we'll see."

Around the same time, I started to pay attention to another staff member, a recreation therapist. Her name was Denise and she rounded us up and led us down the corridor to a room I hadn't previously seen — the exercise room. She put forward the idea that physical health was a key to mental health and our recovery. This echoed what Dr. Brophy had said about physical fitness, and reminded me also of a poster from my brother Erik's bedroom, one that seemed to stay there for years, featuring a downhill skier in a spray of snow and the slogan "A Sound Mind in a Sound Body."

"Do you have any fitness goals, Jan?" Denise asked. She was blond, short, fit. She wore a plaid shirt tucked into her pants. I suspected that she dressed with enthusiasm.

"I want to be tired," I said.

"What do you mean?"

"I want to sleep. That's my biggest problem. I would just like to be very tired, so I can fall asleep tonight."

Rodney, faced with the same query, said he thought that his chest could be bigger, and Denise nodded. That's a good start, I thought. His physique sometimes put me in mind of drought relief programs.

The exercises that Denise had us do often involved two-pound weights or the passing back and forth of inflated rubber balls. She had a big smile and encouraged our efforts, ungainly and unpraiseworthy as they seemed to me.

I waited for my turn on an exercise bike. One was blue, made of what appeared to be tin-snipped metal, and it offered a single gear. The other was the colour of a plastic Band-Aid and I imagined it donated to the hospital in an earlier decade, an act of charity so meagre that it bordered on cruelty. The two small, gripless pedals were set close together and my thighs brushed as I pumped. The cranks also seemed longer than those on my mountain bike, making me sit upright, my knees rising to my chest. A lever on the chassis controlled the amount of resistance on a scale of one to five, and I pushed it to the max, so the band of fabric around the rear wheel tightened, making for an experience not unlike being the prime motive force of some crude generator. The needle of the "speedometer" jittered as it made its way around. I would push that arrow to places the senior citizen who had previously owned this contraption could not have imagined! I rode like fury! Fabric sizzled against plastic! Denise expressed concern that I might overdo it. But I wouldn't be deterred: I would wear down my body, I would pass out from fatigue, my body, my brain. I sat up as straight as I would in an office chair and my legs flew as my kneecaps rose like the pistons in an overtaxed Chevette. We had a half-hour in the room, and I was going to light a small village with the amount of energy

I expended. Meanwhile, Rodney pulled at weights on a cable system, almost pulled back to the wall with each extension from his lats. On the bike next to mine, Ruth, not an agile woman, slid sideways off her seat but maintained her grip on the handlebars until she hung from the side like a trick horse rider at the circus. I kept going. I raced with myself. Fatigue, fatigue, fatigue.

Sleep was the problem. That was what I had somehow lost. People said, you don't appreciate what you have until it's gone, but typically they meant vision or the use of both legs. I'd never imagined a person might lose the gift of naturally falling asleep. Sleep was not easy to appreciate: you had but a hint of its character when drowsing, when reading a book late at night, when words slipped into streams of thought not on the page. You felt sleep when you lacked enough, too. The part it plays in your character suddenly reveals itself, how it buttresses your thoughts and emotions and experience of the world. I felt its absence. I so badly lacked sleep, I no longer recognized myself. Lying awake on a bed in a darkened room was no substitute. That was just a place, and one I dreaded.

Inside me was a broken process, the things that body and brain did together to make sleep, undone. How could I repair it? Keep myself out of that dark, wakeful space? I could visit the exercise room. Exhaust my body. Master the awkward bike. *Sleep, I want you back. I want it to be easy again. A partnership.*

I pedalled.

A GENEROUS LISTENER

NO VISITORS. Michelle and her family had granted this request out of respect for my wishes, and anyway, what was to be gained from telling lots of people I was here? I might have been discharged and on my way to recovery without anyone, really, having to know about this episode of my life. It would have been behind us, and we'd never need to explain it outside of our family.

After my readmission, we re-evaluated. Michelle couldn't keep making up reasons why I wasn't around to take calls from friends. Meanwhile, I surrendered to the idea that I was here, and might stay for a long time. Maybe I would be here until after Christmas. Or maybe I'd keep being discharged and readmitted, like Dorothy and other patients, the "repeats" whose partners needed to bring them back here so they might both have a chance to recuperate. Hard to say what my life would look like from now on, when nobody had a firm idea of what my problem was. I yielded to the idea of staying. I swung between long periods of boredom and intense fits of paranoia. Where else did I belong?

I hadn't imagined the good that seeing friends might do me. They arrived, and suddenly I had allies in the ward. James, my oldest friend, came with his wife. Mary and Dave, too. Maybe this was me here, checked in to a psych ward. That friends didn't seem to mind encouraged me.

"You seem a lot better than you did on Monday," Dave told me.

"Monday," I said.

"Yeah, you seem much more alert today."

"You were here … Monday?"

He must be mistaken. Surely I hadn't seen these two before now …? But nobody contradicted him. I was disturbed. This must have been what Miranda felt like when we told her we couldn't hear any voices from behind the TV.

Something similar occurred at my second ward meeting. The social worker had encouraged us to discuss, as a group, coping methods for our eventual discharge.

"I would like you all to make a list of the people you could call for help, if you find yourself needing it. Let's think. Who is someone you might call?"

"Our minister or clergyman?" I said, eager to display my new-found piety.

"Well, maybe …"

She had in mind people who might actually put us up for the night, if it came to that.

Another exercise was to write down our medications. At the time I took two anti-psychotics, an anti-depressant and an anti-anxiety medicine. This amounted to only four words, and I dutifully copied them down. Presumably if in a few months I stood naked in the parking lot of Kentucky Fried Chicken, trying to produce music from a garbage dumpster, I could hand this list to the person who found me and say, "These are the meds I stopped taking." I should have been able to memorize their names. I knew that, looking at the list, but it would be in my pocket for less than five minutes before the names had slipped my mind and I would have to pull out the scrap of paper. Oh right, Risperdal! Which I would forget almost as soon as I refolded the list. I had blamed the meaninglessness of the names, chosen for sound value and all sounding the same. But Dave's comment made me wonder how severe my mental problems might be. Being unable to read a short story about a Pekingese suffering from flop-bottom was cruel irony. If I couldn't remember basic events over a brief period, life would be awkward when I did get out of here.

Visitors left. They had to leave. More dispiriting, I walked into my room one afternoon to see the psychiatrist, Dr. Whitman, standing next to Rodney's bed, where Rodney sat beside a suitcase that looked suspiciously packed.

"Now Rodney," said Whitman, "when you're at home, don't sit and stare at the computer screen for too long. Okay? The flashing lights ... they can be a trigger."

Rodney nodded, grinning happily.

Flashing lights?

The psychiatrist turned to leave, putting on his hat and touching the brim when he saw me.

At least I could properly wish Rodney luck, as I hadn't managed to do with Angela. Would Rodney and I remain in touch, I wondered, on the outside? I'd buy a ping-pong table, perhaps, or go over to Rodney's house to drink pop and reminisce ...? But it didn't seem like a friendship that could last without extenuating circumstances. We had nothing in common but a need for distraction.

Sad as I was to lose my gangly opponent, I looked forward to having the room to myself. Within an hour, however, a nurse entered the room to strip the sheets and put on fresh ones. The idea of a new roommate further deflated my spirits.

He arrived that evening: Tom, a First Nations fellow with a bruised lip and hair sticking up at the back of his head. He came attached to an IV stand and was the only person I'd seen wearing pyjamas issued by the hospital. I sensed I wouldn't be able to borrow a Bible from him.

He seemed to feel the awkwardness of an uninvited guest. I gave as much welcome as I could in my paranoid state.

"Let's see," I said. "You can get clean towels from that rack by the nurses' station. Oh, make sure you fill out the chits after lunch and dinner so you can choose your meal for the next day. And you can help yourself to juice or whatever's in the fridge."

In the evening, lying in our beds, we pulled privacy curtains around us. My bed was between Tom's and our shared bathroom. As I lay, I heard him shuffling along, carrying his IV stand through the narrow space as one might carry a small Christmas tree, knocking it noisily against the leg of my bed.

"Sorry, Jan!" he whispered.

"No problem."

He went into the washroom and soon I heard him cursing behind the door, presumably encountering the challenge of taking a leak while connected to an IV tube and wearing unfamiliar pyjamas. I offered no advice. It still beat listening to Rodney talk in his sleep.

With Rodney gone, I looked for other candidates to benefit from my association with them. Tom's IV tube made for too much of a handicap in ping-pong, even if the other player was me. There was Ruth. Ruth had been a near constant during both of my stays. She could frustrate even Bernard with her capacity for talk — I had seen her do it, and it had improved her standing with me. I had generally avoided people whom I thought might question me, but eventually realized this was no worry with Ruth. She could keep both ends of a conversation going. I could view her as somebody's harmless eccentric aunt, and I gave her the opportunity to wear me down with talk.

"Nobody has ever said how birds manage to find their way north and south each year, with the seasons. Maybe they can feel weather patterns in a way we can't, maybe it's the magnetism of the Earth and they have a way of sensing it and using it to guide them, I don't know."

Ducks had landed in the pond outside. It was December; they should have been gone. I realized something new from our brief conversation and later approached the male nurse. "Ruth is smart," I said.

"Hm? Oh, Ruth. Yeah, she's bright. I think she has her Ph.D. in something or other. She was a very smart woman. Then one day her family found her living in the back seat of her car."

I started to seek her out. "Tell me more about the superiority of the Roman baths." She was full of information. True, she didn't know when to quit, and she might discuss the mating habits of tapeworms after I had just lifted the lid from my beef stroganoff, but she was less offensive than the television in the lounge. Ruth's ramblings soothed, somehow. I could listen to her talk. And as with Rodney, I felt as if I performed an act of charity on behalf of another human being, when actually, it was I who benefited.

MARRING A CHOIR

THE PROBLEM WITH READING troubled me. If I couldn't read, what could I do? Who was I, with that subtracted from the sum of me? Our home was full of books. My workplace, too, and the career I had imagined.

I had much time to kill and knew that I couldn't get anywhere, least of all home, if I didn't make an effort.

From that box my brother had mailed me, I chose another title: *The Evolution of Useful Things* by Henry Petroski. A non-fiction book, it featured on the cover an enlarged image of a fingertip on which a paper clip balanced, plus a small patent diagram illustrating the same object. The title of the first chapter, "How the Fork Got Its Tines," implied what I hoped to find within, a lively and surprising investigation into commonplace objects, with little or no conflict. I wanted to enjoy it and I wanted to retain what I read. The text was more challenging than a James Herriot story, to be sure, but the combination of historical anecdote, commonplace objects and progressive, rational redesign seemed somehow promising. I read the book in my room to minimize distractions and I tried not to fret whenever I noticed my grasp on the material was slipping. It was an effort.

"What are you reading?"

Dr. Brophy appeared at the foot of my bed. I'd only heard the click of shoe heels in the hall. I shut the book quickly and put it on my bedside table.

"*The Evolution of Useful Things*," I said. "It's interesting." Clumsily I knocked over my cup of water, forcing me to relocate the book and dry the spillage with my towel.

"Useful things like Styrofoam cups?" he said.

"Right."

"I thought I'd check in on you before the weekend," he said.

He ran through a truncated set of questions as to how I was doing; I didn't mention my problem with reading, but I could report success in another regard.

"I've been talking to other patients, like you said."

"Which patients?"

"Rodney, before he left. And Ruth."

"Hm," he said.

He left soon after. His tone made me wonder if he didn't consider Ruth a good conversationalist; he had sounded no more enthusiastic about Styrofoam cups. When I had finished mopping up the water, I looked at my own cup. Admittedly, a Styrofoam cup could be awkward. Its lightness made it easy to spill, and like anyone, I wanted to barf if an empty one bumped against me in a body of water. But there was something great, too, about a houseware that you could use once or a thousand times and feel you had gotten your money's worth, that you had no particular obligation to after you finished knocking it over, that came off its stack in predictable shape and state of cleanliness, guaranteed to have touched no human hands (or other appendages) before your own. And what about the perfect mailing box holding the items Gail sent me? How much less appealing would the contents have been in a shoebox with the name of the farm written on the lid in felt pen? The apple cider and mug could lift the spirits of people around the world because of that smart container.

I found the last paragraph I could remember in my book and resumed reading.

NOW THAT DENISE, the recreation therapist, had made a connection, she wouldn't quit. "Hey, Mr. Writer, sitting there all by yourself. You too busy to help us make Christmas trees out of old newspapers?"

Some people have therapeutic personalities. I sensed no faking in her smile: she seemed honestly delighted to see someone measuring ingredients for muffins. She again proclaimed the benefits of daily exercise, though she didn't think exercise should be performed so vigorously that you couldn't maintain a conversation at the same time.

As I well knew, the ward looked into a courtyard, and here Denise could herd a sizable group of us. A lack of appropriate clothing was no excuse to be left out, as she could always rummage through the lost-and-found box for a toque or fluorescent orange sweater, and no citing of fashion trends could discourage her. We walked.

In many cities, this much green space would have qualified as a park. An adjacent seniors' facility shared the courtyard but I never saw anyone but psych patients and CIA marksmen on the grounds.

Denise prodded us along. She kept everybody moving on the paved trails, some people better walkers than others. The group got ahead of me; I was by far the slowest. Ruth in her housecoat and toque could manage a faster waddle. I had noticed my plodding gait earlier, on a day pass.

"Come on, Jan!" Denise called, looking back at me with a smile. "Keep those legs moving!"

I tried to. I watched the group toddle ahead. She busily kept people from wandering away, while also pointing out the koi, et cetera. I didn't like being a straggler.

"Hey there slowpoke," she called back happily a few minutes later. "Shake a leg."

Keeping up should not have been a challenge. Strange, I wanted my legs to move faster, but they didn't respond. They swung stiffly. My stride was abbreviated. And it worsened. The muscles of my limbs tightened, making the process harder, no longer a gait but a lurch. The stiffening spread to my neck, my arms, my jaw. How much slower could I get? I swung my wooden limbs, but there was no bend any more. I wasn't working, but kept moving forward. I toppled.

I lay on the ground. Couldn't get up, either. I was wound so tight that I couldn't so much as flop.

I saw the texture of the asphalt, the pebbles, the path. The distant crowd of misfits who were my peers. Enjoying the pond, the gazebo. Ruth's toque sitting atop her head like a pylon. Tom had come with his IV stand. Soon Denise would look back to check my progress. Wasn't it time to cajole me again? *Come on, Denise, look.* I watched her, waited; I saw her turn her head. Strange to wait for someone's expression to change.

"Omigod, Jan!" She ran back to me and squatted. "Are you okay?! Can you talk?"

"Seized. Up."

"Okay, okay, here, let's get you onto a bench."

Bernard came limping speedily toward me; my eyes widened. He and Denise helped to right me and drag me to a bench. In other circumstances his touch would have elicited a shout, but my face had locked: I could hardly speak. They pulled me over and propped me on the bench, upright, with my legs straight out before me as if I were merely taking a moment to relax and stare at the trees with a frozen rictus.

"I know what's happening," said Denise. "Don't worry, don't worry, I know what's happening!"

She sprinted to the ward. Her words seemed at odds with her manner, but I opted to listen to the words. Here was Bernard, standing nearby in a way that could almost be described as protective. The other patients drifted back to the bench to stand around, too. Tom, someone I drank eggnog with, someone who had let me back into the ward after yet another of my melodramatic exits. These people had seen me in unflattering situations. And here they stood, my posse of fellow mental patients. "You're going to be all right," Ruth pronounced, wearing her toque, bringing up the rear. At least I had their support. It was support.

Denise banged out the doors with a wheelchair. She loaded me into it and wheeled me quickly back into the unit.

"You're having a reaction to one of your meds," she said. "But you're going to be fine."

With the assistance of a nurse, she deposited me onto my bed, where I lay, face down.

"You're going to be okay," Denise repeated, sounding upset. "The nurse will be back here in a few minutes."

Soon I heard footsteps and the weak elastic snap of latex gloves going on. I recognized the nurse's voice.

"You're having a reaction to your anti-psychotic," she told me. "I've got a shot here for you; it'll work faster if I give it to you in the posterior."

"Go for it," I said into the pillow.

The shot of benztropine would restore balance to the chemicals in my body. She said, "That should only take a few minutes to work. Don't get out of bed right away though, Jan, because your legs might still be affected. Just sit up, and I'll come help you."

"Thanks."

I lay, waiting for the benztropine to circulate. The nurse had seemed almost bored and I chose to take that as a reassuring sign. I just had to wait for my muscles to come back under my control. Actually this was less pressure than trying to keep up with the group in the yard.

I was restored by the time Michelle came to visit me that evening, but this didn't lessen her dismay upon learning what had happened. I heard her speaking in urgent tones at the nursing station.

Denise's standing with me rose. I looked forward to her appearances on the ward. One afternoon, those of us who could be trusted with paintbrushes stood before a big white sheet of poster paper that covered a dining table. Somebody's daughter, an art student in high school, had pencilled a picture of a choir of angels, and we were to colour in their stylized torsos, wings and halos, not only killing an hour or so of the drudgery of ward life, but also, in the process, making a decoration for the walls, something to prop our spirits as we waited for a holiday season in care. The excellence of the drawing was oft noted. As I worked, I thought about the girl who had sketched these heavenly figures, and other art projects. The nurses spoke as if she herself were a kind of angel. Had her mother pressed her into service? Or did she volunteer her skills? Was art her thing?

I had failed to notice one of the lines in the illustration. The shoulder of my angel now merged with the sky.

"Damn it!" I said. "What an idiot I am. Maybe I better let someone else take over for me."

Denise hurried to my side. "Oh, Jan, don't worry about it — really, it's okay! Nobody will notice, and anyway, it doesn't matter. Really, don't worry."

She may have overestimated my inner torment for having made this mistake. I understood that as the recreation therapist, Denise was a low woman on the totem pole of health care providers at the hospital. What I didn't appreciate, or at least couldn't at the time articulate appreciating, was how many of my usual concerns I was not contemplating, thanks to her and her projects. Even delusional, I could not cast Denise in the role of government operative. It just didn't seem credible that an agent would be so keen to have us bake muffins. She could draw me into conversation and make it positive no matter where I started from.

In better control of my body, I reattempted the courtyard.

Denise knew features that I would have ignored had it been just another green space that I walked while sane, like the curved wall, designed so that if you stood on the spot marked by a green tile and spoke, you would hear your voice projected at volume. We each took a turn at this amusement, which, in those other times, I would have found slight. We stood on wooden platforms and peered down into the pond for a flash of goldfish, or the rumoured turtles, or just looked at the lilies stretching in natural pattern across the surface. It was great to be outside, among willow and fir trees, and they too were great. Nobody was hiding behind them. All the trees and bushes did, really, was enclose the space and make privacy, so a person could come out here without seeing cars on the street or who drove them. It was a space where a person might take a break from things going on in his or her head. The foliage didn't hide marksmen or federal agents; rather, it helped hide my affliction and me from society at large.

Inside, the painting of the choir hung on the wall, the geometric mouths of angels open wide to sing from their geometric hymnals. I couldn't look at the painting without noticing my gimpy contribution, the one singer with her shoulder fused to the sky. The important thing, though, was that Christmas remained some time away, and things appeared better for me getting out. Once discharged, I could pick my psychiatrist. My choice would be Whitman, so as I continued to see Brophy, this knowledge added what felt like a layer of falsity to our conversations.

My condition had improved. I told him so, but of course, I had told him this before.

"I think we'll be sending you home in the next day or two," he said.

"That's great," I said.

I felt pleased; he too seemed satisfied. This struck me as a good end to the conversation and an opportunity to get out of the office before he could change his mind. Thankfully he hadn't asked me about the Bible again. But I thought of other books on my bedside table, the taxing *Evolution of Useful Things*, the equally difficult James Herriot dog stories with their surrealist imagery, as well as the abandoned P. G. Wodehose novel, *It's Impenetrable, Jeeves!*, or whatever it was called.

Should I mention my problems reading? And risk adding another three or four days to my stay? Should I let the truth be my guide? Or my guardian, or my lantern? Or, should I just keep my mouth shut?

"There is one thing," I said. "Reading. I find it difficult."

"What about reading?"

"I have a hard time. I can't remember things I've just read. I forget, almost immediately. Simple things like the names of characters. I read something and it just evaporates."

"It's the medication," he said. "It's not unlike being drunk. That will wear off, eventually."

"What a relief," I said.

And the meeting ended, with no more discussion and perhaps only an extra perfunctory line on my chart.

PART FOUR

Useful Things

THE APOLOGY MAKER

MY SECOND HOMECOMING was tainted by its secondness.

I hadn't imagined after my first discharge that I might return to the ward so quickly, and the possibility of going back a third time lingered. The hospital staff seemed to think that I need stay no longer, but no one pretended I was "right," and being back in the apartment brought that fact home to me. Or rather, brought that fact to our home.

Five days a week I would attend a program run by the hospital for outpatients. I would also see Dr. Whitman outside of that setting. My diagnosis could best be summarized by my pills: Alprazolam, Doxepin, and Risperdal. Anti-anxiety, anti-depressant, anti-psychotic.

I was off work. Dr. Brophy had written a note — just two sentences, models of economy yet broadly forgiving — to excuse me from my duties at the library, and though I felt guilty receiving sick pay for a condition wanting in physical symptoms, I knew I could not stand behind the counter and resume wanding barcodes. I couldn't face anyone. Because of my aberrant behaviour when I was last in the branch, I had a hard time seeing myself back in that setting, as if nothing had happened. Something *had* happened there. I had crossed a line. I had done so in public, in a place where I had established a certain character to match my role, and the breakdown, apart from being humiliating, felt like a betrayal of my place in the picture. How many patrons knew? Had Gail been required to explain to people what happened, or apologize on my behalf? Would patrons still feel ours was a library they could safely bring children to, knowing that a mental case was checking out their books? I didn't want to be a source of discomfort. I dreaded awkward conversation. I was better off in the apartment. Everyone was.

Michelle's employers let her change her hours so that she could drive me to and from the outpatient program. We had a second car but I didn't trust myself to operate it. I would kill someone. I would fall asleep at the wheel or forget what a red light meant and not come to a stop until bodies got caught up in the axle.

I maintained a residual paranoia about the end of the world and the end of our personal world. Would the novel instigate a series of calamities? Or, at least, would it ruin the cushy domestic routines centred on this apartment? When Michelle was at work, I could go into my office and look at the novel in various forms. The galleys. My manuscript with notes. Reference materials. I wondered if Harcourt would proceed with publication, and felt profoundly ambivalent.

In my office I also stared at my books and my handcrafted Hanuman mask and a dangly blue souvenir of Turkey intended to ward off the evil eye. Mostly my books. I would take one from the shelf and look at its cover, try to read a few pages. I couldn't. Usually I gave up and waited, standing near the door, already on the verge of tears when Michelle got home from work.

"I know these are my favourite books," I said to her. "But I look around my office and none of it means anything to me. I don't care about any of it. It's nothing to me."

I had lost my love for everything I owned, everything I had arranged with such care on the shelves or tacked up on the walls. I didn't care to revisit *The Handmaid's Tale*, nor watch my Kat clock switch its eyes back and forth, nor smirk at my Mexican lobby cards of '50s monster movies — *El Monstruo Asesino* and *Guerra de la Bestia Humana*. A one-eyed giant hurling a bus, in lurid colours — that was amusing, wasn't it? Shouldn't I see it as funny? *Una Horrible Criatura, Engendro de los Infiernos!* These items defined me; I found them devoid of appeal.

In the evenings I clung. Though no help in the kitchen, I would follow Michelle back and forth, a pace behind her in that small space. She had discovered an Australian daytime soap called *A Country Practice* in the upper reaches of our cable selection and we watched taped episodes every evening after dinner, although I could muster little concern for whose wallaby was struck by whose utility vehicle and the many other storylines weaving in and out of Wandin Valley Hospital.

Time bothered me. Watching that show or a video, I'd feel as if an hour must have passed since it began. But when I looked at my watch, I would see, to my frustration, that only ten minutes had elapsed. I checked the clock often and my irritation grew. Descriptions of depression told me that its sufferers "lack concentration," but to me it felt as if time dragged at a slower than normal rate, as if screws had been tightened on the hands of a universal clock. It was painful, how slowly an evening could creep by. I just wanted whatever was happening to be over.

Depression was the tag that had stuck with me since that nurse suggested it. A psychotic depression, and yes, I did cry with guilt when Michelle came home, and I wanted nothing but to go to bed and to sleep, deep, dreamless, medicated sleep, the one state in which I didn't feel time's awful torpor. After waking in the morning, I would lie in bed, hoping to drift into another hour of unconsciousness. All of this fit with depression. Sleep disturbances were a typical symptom, as were sudden crying jags and a fixation with death. Had that resident doctor to whom I complained about my insomnia and cyst been more perceptive, he might have suspected depression, or some mental problem. Oh, well. Once I had glimpsed him following Dr. Fisk through the ward; they didn't speak to me. Maybe the resident would be better informed for next time. That was the purpose of being a resident, I supposed. But thinking back, I can also understand Dr. Brophy's hesitation to diagnose depression in me. At the time of my first admission to the unit, I had not been uninterested in life: I had maybe been *too* interested. I hadn't felt time's slow tick. I wasn't passive. I was sad occasionally. The symptoms didn't really hit until I found myself out of the ward.

One thing we did know: it wasn't just the old man who had lived down the road from us in a single filthy room of his mansion, or the guy who did jumping jacks in the library, or the woman who, every day, had come to the video store where I worked in junior high so she could ask my boss to set up a machine in the back for her daily viewing of *Love Me Tender*. They were mentally ill. I was mentally ill. I had realized it. I belonged to the same club as they did, it was me, too: it had happened to me.

Why?

PSYCHIATRY WAS TRICKY, and so too were its drugs. My symptoms changed, my medicines were rejigged; one altered the other. My speech was slurred, my handwriting illegible. Was that my condition, or a side effect? My face felt frozen, I forgot what had been said minutes before. My steps were sluggish, I seized up badly on a walk. A symptom might bring on a new prescription, crossing one med off the list to make room for another, and it was impossible to predict how drugs might interact in one individual or another. I could appreciate this. Out of the ward, I tried to see chemical reactions for what they were. I had a hard time begrudging the anti-psychotic, Risperdal, if it would reduce my tendency to see air-conditioning repairmen as gun-wielding federal agents. Later I would suspect it came with a side effect unique to me.

Immediately after my second discharge, I was more concerned with the desertification of my body. I had never felt so dry before. My eyes were dry, my fingers papery. My plumbing was so slow I worried I would "go septic," as I'd heard a senior citizen describe it, and found myself anxiously tearing into Costco-sized bags of prunes. Most days I would sit inside the apartment and do nothing but further dehydrate myself with tears as I contemplated the ways I had ruined my wife's life.

My depression, Dr. Whitman suggested, might be exacerbated by another medication: impossible to know. I would make the bed or force myself to clean the bathroom. People encouraged me to go for walks, and I would drag myself outside and set my goal as the end of the street, and hate every step, and turn back early, and get inside and vow to never inflict that misery upon myself again. One of the few tasks involving human interaction that I attempted was buying groceries. I walked across the road, back to Safeway.

The glare of lights remained. My mental state was better than during my last trip here, but I still felt quietly scrutinized. I dreaded going to the checkout to find I was unable to count change, or even pluck it from that small, awkward, velcroed pocket of my wallet. My goal was to buy a few apples. Just a few apples, but I couldn't get the bag open. With difficulty I ripped one of those flimsy produce department bags off the roll, then stood and tried to open one end, and, when it offered more resistance than I could face, the other end. My fingers were so dry that the plastic sides preferred to stay closed. I rubbed and rubbed. I knew the motion, but the meagre reward of seeing the plastic gain a mouth and part wide enough to admit three apples wouldn't come. Minutes ticked on the huge Safeway clock. I rubbed my fingertips against the cheap plastic with the intensity of a man trying to start a fire in freezing weather. No luck. I retried the other end of the bag. There seemed a good chance a produce clerk would approach and ask me to leave the store. There was a real chance that I would burst into tears.

I got back home. I must have, eventually, but I probably didn't sit on the couch eating apples if I did succeed in buying them. I sat and waited for Michelle to come home so I could tell her the latest apology I had been working on. I might glance at my room. I had bought hundreds of books over the years with the intention of reading them someday, when I had spare time, but this was not the day, nor would tomorrow be the day. Didn't look good for next week, nor for the months ahead. Time was abundant, awful. I didn't want anything except for this to be over. Why? Why was I like this?

Michelle had not taken my admission to the unit lightly. She had mobilized and solicited opinions from all of her acquaintances in the field of mental health. The most profitable call was to her friend's brother, a psychiatrist named Johannes Giede.

"When you were getting ready for your trip to India," he'd asked, "did you take any anti-malarial medication?"

We had taken one, mefloquine, though we knew it by its trade name, Lariam. Somehow this question had been missed at the hospital during my first admission, but it was one of the first things Giede asked.

Mefloquine, an effective preventative treatment for malaria, can also cause psychiatric symptoms including hallucinations and psychosis. In 1992 some famously ugly episodes in Somalia severely tarnished the reputation of a Canadian airborne regiment sent there as part of a UN relief mission. Later it emerged that the regiment members had been required to take mefloquine, and many of them came to describe the nights following their pills as "nightmare Wednesdays." Hearing the soldiers describe their symptoms — nightmares, anxiety, depression, sleeplessness — I felt real recognition. Lariam has no doubt saved many lives from malaria, but side effects may have driven some people to suicide attempts and psychotic behaviour.

Could Lariam have been my smoking gun? A smoking pill? Taking the drug had coincided exactly with the surprising, intense fear of flying that had scuttled our India trip, and I remembered feeling like a different and unstable person at that time. The idea fit with my whole experience: successes had become disasters, comforts came to haunt me and a pill, one more reversal, the source of it all, something meant to protect me instead fucked me up. Once it was mentioned at the hospital, mefloquine was incorporated into my diagnosis, though when I asked the psychiatrist, he avoided declaring it the lone cause, preferring to suggest that it might have been a possible trigger. I disliked the looseness of such replies, craving specific answers and new rules to apply to my life.

I too was reluctant to place all blame on the anti-malarial. My psychotic episode and suicide plans had occurred sometime after taking Lariam; we had stopped the course of medication as soon as our plans fell apart. Could it have remained in my system that long? Weeks? If it was designed to protect a person from the disease for a lengthy period, could potential side effects linger, too — nightmarish paranoid thoughts sitting unhatched, like malaria parasites sitting in the liver and multiplying, waiting to act? I wasn't sure.

What good would it do, anyway, to declare Lariam the culprit? There was no antidote for the side effects. Nothing could reverse the depression, the paranoia, the anxiety, after they took hold. These disorders had to be treated with more drugs, or nothing. I would sit in book-deprived isolation, in irrational misery, waiting and hoping but not believing that I might someday improve.

THE OREO DIET

I SAW DR. WHITMAN every two weeks or so, and between appointments attended an outpatient program for depressives who emerged from the ward and elsewhere. The "Day Program" was offered as a step toward recovery, with staff that had specialized knowledge about depression and access to hospital resources. I didn't want to go. I didn't want to do *anything*, even something I knew might help me. Motivation was absent. On a practical level, my participation would allow Michelle to go to work without fretting about what I did with my copious and dismal free time, and this as much as anything persuaded me to make the effort. The program was provided at the hospital, only a short spell of pacing down the hall from the psych ward. In the space between, psychiatrists had offices, as did the nurses whom I'd soon meet, and though I could look down to see those orange doors and the yellowish '70s brickwork, this end of the hall fell under the Expo 86 colour scheme, the doors a medicinal teal.

On one door, a computer printout read: "You are responsible to do your own dishes." On the walls hung tired-looking mental health awareness posters, plus a chalkboard. As I waited for the first session to begin, a collage caught my attention.

I suspected patients before me had created this work, with roughly snipped magazine photos and headlines glued onto a piece of cheapish white poster paper. The theme puzzled me. A collage should have a caption to explain itself, shouldn't it? The problem here was too many captions, extracted from the pages of *Sunset* or *Canadian Living*. "Tears of Pity, Tears of Hate." "This Cramp's For You." Given the setting, the assignment had probably been to highlight the many stressors of daily life that might eventually lead someone into this place, this very spot, where he could do little but stand and stare at a collage. "Colon cancer." "Tug of war." "Gum disease." A picture of an old man who seemed very lonely, judging by his expression and the harsh lighting. A dirty sink full of dishes. "Overweight child," "Child abuse." The closeness of those two made me wonder if overweight child abuse was a problem for anyone. As I continued to look over the sun-faded, glue-rippled expanse, I began to question my guess of the theme. "Schoolyard bullying." "Bad breath." "Flea market." Flea market? Well, I could see how flea markets could be a source of stress in people's lives. Certainly I'd felt a discomfort that might be called stress on the few occasions I had entered the big weekly flea market at the exhibition grounds. If someone felt compelled to shop there, to buy his or her wardrobe and Christmas gifts there, oh yeah, that did make sense. But not far from "flea market" and pictures of a bathroom scale and a homeless man was one of a monkey sitting on the back of an Airedale terrier, apparently grooming him. This might have been stressful for the dog ... Actually he appeared unfazed. Was it a metaphor? Neither could I understand the inclusion of the word "leprechauns" in the hodgepodge, and a quick survey revealed not one but three depictions of heavenly babies. Not cherubs in the classical sense,

I believe these were the angelic results of children who had died without sin: one image of winged, haloed, cloud-inhabiting innocents appearing in an advertisement for porcelain dolls, one cartoon, and one realistic rendering, though I suppose "naturalistic" is the slightly more accurate term.

A man came down the hallway to unlock the door. "Here for the Day Program?"

"Yes."

"You must be Jan."

I was, and still found the fact disappointing. A number of nurses facilitated the program but we would most often see this chipper fellow, Gary, who let me into the small room where daily meetings took place. Maybe I had seen Gary hovering about the ward during my stay. I sat at the table and tried to evade his questions about writing. Not what I wanted to talk about. The last thing I wanted to talk about. Didn't want to talk about anything.

Another man came in, looking sad. He wore blue coveralls or perhaps matching blue trousers and jacket, with oil stains, and he managed to say hello to Gary and me before dropping into his chair to contract upon himself. We learned his name was Joe. Joe stared at a point in the faux-wood-grain tabletop.

The third patient to enter wore a puffy nylon winter jacket and glasses of the auto-tinting variety, still darkened by the morning chill. He carried a stack of Oreos in one hand and a coffee in the other. Gary greeted him as Antoine. Though I saw him five times a week he always seemed to be sporting three days' growth of beard.

Gary said, "Found the cookies, I see!"

"Breakfast," said Antoine.

And this was it. This was the sum of our group. I had expected maybe a dozen or so people, but it was late December and the slacker attitudes toward all things seemed to include the Day Program. Gary introduced it and gave us handouts, detailing our responsibilities. We were obliged to try to attend every day and complete all "homework." For their part, the staff wouldn't greet us if they saw us outside of the hospital, in, say, A Buck or Two, so as not to remind us in public of our bleak situation. Gary prodded each of us into sharing a little about ourselves and our circumstances.

Joe, the fellow in the blue outfit, was a self-employed upholsterer who specialized in boats. He made a passable living at it, not great money, but recently found himself unable to face his work, and worried about the people who had brought him their boats and were waiting for their refurbished seats and armrests.

"Do you have an assistant who helps you?" asked Gary.

"No. Sometimes my wife."

"Can she do some of the work for you? If you gave her tips?"

"No, no, it's beyond her abilities, really. I just worry about those people who are expecting their work to get done. They won't wait forever."

I got anxious too, thinking about his predicament. Nobody who visited the library would care if someone else scanned the barcodes on their books, but all those boats ... I could well imagine the backlog, watercraft sitting in a yard in various states of disassembly, and I could tell from Joe's affect that nothing could be done about it. Gary eventually gave up trying to suggest ways for him to get around the situation.

What Antoine did for a living I never really learned, but he was the first person I met whose depression manifested itself in anger control problems. He was quite helpful in showing me the kitchen next door, where we were responsible to do our own dishes and could find free juice and cookies, and sometimes his kids would show up on their way to or from school to fill their pockets. Once I saw the boy, age ten, pouring himself a coffee. I wondered what a household managed by Antoine might look like. "Yeah, I got in a bit of trouble back in Edmonton," he told me one day. "Didn't like something my boss said. So I set his truck on fire."

I wasn't eager to share too much about my situation, and summarized it with the handy half-truth that I was a writer and the approaching publication of my book had caused great stress that had ultimately brought me here. I appreciated the staff not greeting me in public but I was more concerned that my relationship with Antoine not extend far outside these walls.

It must be said that this was not an easy group to facilitate. "Good morning!" Gary would say, coming into the room, and nobody would reply; in fact it was another miserable morning but none of us had the energy to inform him of that. We had nothing to offer. We brought not a shred of interest in the activity planned for the day, or any activity, and could not summon what might be viewed as a base level of polite faked enthusiasm.

We seemed to run out of new ways to pass our time together rather quickly. There was a wipe-board in the room and on the first day, Gary drew a picture of a synapse like those that might be found in a brain, with an explanation of the role of neurotransmitters, and how ours might not be working, and how our anti-depressants could help. It was a good picture but Gary was a little too fond of making it. He always seemed to want to draw it. Sometimes he seemed to be talking about a different topic and yet the synapse picture would emerge on the board. Other times, one of many dead pauses would arise in the discussion, and he would go and put a squiggle on the board. I recognized the squiggle as the beginning of a synapse. Maybe he was like my mother, who knew how to draw just one animal, and in response to me begging her to draw a monkey, could only do her owl and add limbs and a tail.

Repetition frustrated me; I had the feeling that time had slowed to scrape at my sanity. On the unit, I had been shown a video about depression co-hosted by John Cleese and a British physician with a bad stoop. The first time I had recognized the video as amusing, even if I couldn't laugh. The second time it had seemed like an annoying infomercial, a series of canned moments of would-be humour. When Gary set up a video machine with a promise that we were about to enjoy an informative program by a pair of hilarious British guys, I got up in a huff and told him I was leaving, phoning Michelle to come from work and pick me up. "I can't watch that again."

Gary could accept this.

On another morning, the topic was perfectionism. To what degree was it responsible for spoiling our lives?

"When you're redoing those boats," Gary said to Joe, "do you feel compelled to get the job done perfectly?"

"Of course I try to do the best job possible, and some of the work is fine, but I wouldn't say it gets as far as perfectionism."

"But you are a perfectionist."

"No, I'm not a perfectionist."

"Jan," Gary said, turning to me, "when you're writing, do you try to get the words exactly right? Do you feel as if you can't stop until you've got the story or novel perfect?"

"I do a lot of rewriting. I try to polish the work before I start submitting it, but I wouldn't flatter myself by calling it perfectionism."

Gary turned to look at Antoine. He paused. I could understand his difficulty in putting the question to him. *Antoine, when you're setting fire to somebody's car or truck, do you feel compelled to make sure that the gasoline is spread over the entire vehicle, getting the hood and the cab all doused, so the whole thing goes up in one nice* whumpf? In the end Gary opted to ask him nothing and move on.

At the outset we'd filled out a sheet of questions like those asked by the ward's admitting nurses, intended to gauge the level of our depression. The sheets looked like fourth-generation photocopies, each consecutive copy having thickened the letters and added stray marks, errant grains of toner representing errant static, and an eyelash of a mark that appeared on the same place every page, probably the machine's interpretation of a scratch on the glass bed. Nevertheless, staff took the sheets seriously. Was I crying more often than normal? Yes. Was I having recurrent thoughts of death? I couldn't deny imagining the painful demise of John Cleese and his sidekick.

When this dipstick of my mental health was checked a month or so into the program, Gary quickly got up to confer with the other staff and they decided to call my psychiatrist, as the results suggested I had become more depressed, not less.

Useful things came out of the program. We would be shepherded to a larger room to lie on mats and listen to relaxation tapes, and I was glad to take these home — one more tool in the search for natural sleep. Sometimes my fellow patients wouldn't show up, and the staff-to-me ratio would be even smaller. Denise might appear to prod me into going on another walk. "You've lived here all your life and never watched the curlers before? Well get your jacket, we're going to the curling club!" Or: "You've lived here all your life and never been to the museum before? Put your jacket on, we're going to the museum!" To me, the walk sounded unbearably long, but she seemed able to shorten the distance between points A and B, and somehow minimize the experience of traffic.

One day a staff member placed on the table before us glue sticks, scissors and a stack of old magazines, and I knew what was coming. Privately I questioned the therapeutic value of the collage. I suspected the true reason it had arisen in this setting was its valuable role as time-killer, as well as being almost necessitated by the availability of the materials.

"Today we're making a food collage," said the worker. "I want you to go through the magazines for pictures of the sort of foods that make up your diet."

Antoine looked at the stack of magazines as if she'd placed a saucer of urine in front of him. I at least would make an effort, even if I felt the exercise was more remedial than necessary. I suspected that it was really a ploy to start a certain discussion, one guided by our decisions to adorn the paper with images of whole wheat bread or tubes of Pillsbury cookie dough. It didn't look as if Antoine would participate. The problem for me was not so much that I didn't know what foods fit into a healthy diet but the fact that these magazines had been used as a source of material before. The pages flipped over in that limp way pages do when pictures are missing.

"The Food Guide says you should be eating vegetables at least five times a day," said our facilitator during the ensuing discussion.

"I don't eat vegetables," said Antoine.

"None?"

"Nah."

"Do you find they're too much trouble to prepare?"

"Too expensive," he said.

"Carrots aren't expensive. You can buy a big bag of carrots for three bucks."

He leaned back, balancing on his chair. "Naah."

There was always something. Always some reason why change was impossible for Antoine. What was the matter with this guy? The focus of my irritation could shift from staff members to anybody else on the thinnest pretext. Did he like the way his life was? Didn't he want to get better?

Sometimes his offspring, having raided the cookie stash, would be standing in the hall waiting for him when we finished for the day. Our group met on Antoine's birthday, too; somehow the date of it had come up in conversation the prior week and Gary had remembered.

"Anyone do anything special for you this morning?" he asked Antoine.

"Nope."

"Kids didn't surprise you with breakfast in bed?"

"Jan said happy birthday. He's the only person."

I shrank in my seat.

"Well, happy birthday!"

With the blessing of my physician, I had started driving to the program, and not only had I so far avoided slaying any pedestrians with our Civic, but I also felt glad to relieve Michelle of the duty of carting me back and forth. I had never imagined that operating a car could feel like such an accomplishment. One afternoon, finished for the day, Antoine and I walked out together.

"Parked way down there, eh?" he said.

"Yeah."

"Check it out."

He nodded at his car. It was a dark brown Chevelle with rusted wheel wells and a patina of soil. It looked as if Edmonton had been as unkind to his vehicle as it had to Antoine. Some of that grime had definitely been carried across the Rockies. But the point was his parking spot, right outside the hospital in the fifteen-minute zone.

"Alberta plates," he said. "They can write as many tickets as they want but they got no way to fine me."

I made some comment that conveyed a satisfactory level of envy before we parted, and I got behind the wheel of our mostly clean, relatively new car. Driving was something. It was a sign of improvement that I thought I could do this, and maybe time's passing or the boosted anti-depressant was responsible. The Day Program? Often it amounted to daycare for the depressed, but that was valuable to Michelle and me, and the fact that any program existed for such a miserable group of people was something to credit. If nothing else it made me realize that however piteous I felt, I had met Antoine, someone whose head state was as bad as mine but who had little going for him beyond out-of-province plates.

A CAN OPENER FOR OUR TIMES

I KEPT WORKING AT READING, and one day, I found a book that clicked: *The Discoverers* by Daniel J. Boorstin. I'd picked it up during our train trip across Canada but put it aside while editing the novel. Boorstin's book is a sweeping survey of the progress of scientific exploration. And, I could read it. If I read slowly and reread when necessary, the ideas stuck, and my excitement over this accomplishment rivalled that of Magellan upon crossing the Pacific.

Most of the credit lies with Boorstin. His writing and approach to the subject matter could engage even a mentally ill person, and the book was different enough from my usual reading material that I stumbled upon few chutes leading back down to my state of nervous paranoia. It was all ladders. As with *The Evolution of Useful Things*, I found *The Discoverers* more manageable than the easiest elementary-school fiction, and I wondered what made the difference. Maybe fiction has a reputation as being frivolous, more obviously written for entertainment value than non-fiction. Serious people read non-fiction, after all. But non-fiction books can accommodate readers who drop in and out of their breadth. A person can still derive something useful from a fragment:

maybe that's what made non-fiction easier for me, with my perforated concentration. The steps up which Boorstin takes the reader are incremental, discoveries building upon prior discoveries, but one can enjoy individual anecdotes: Marco Polo's meeting with Kublai Khan, say, or sea captains hiding early versions of the compass from superstitious sailors, for their own sake. A novel, on the other hand, a good novel, expects you to carry through with characters to the end. There's a pleasure that derives solely from the long arc of the narrative. You want to feel a kind of foreshadowing in early chapters, and have it satisfied through the middle and ending, even if you never articulate what that is. Maybe that was why I couldn't derive any pleasure from *The Mad Scientists' Club* or *James and the Giant Peach*.

I had never ventured into the self-help section of a bookstore. As with Disney movies and Aussie soaps, though, now seemed a good time to relax my standards. A book recommended to me was *Feeling Good: The New Mood Therapy* by David D. Burns. I appreciated that it made no grand claims in the title, but the cover — text in a large, easy-to-read typeface, in colours somehow suggestive of an intention to solve problems — still made me sceptical. I gave it a try. Most of what I read seemed sound advice, but I most benefited from a single word that I had not previously encountered.

The word was "catastrophize." It was listed among the types of mental processes that depressed persons tended toward and that needed correction. I had been doing it for months with my compulsive doomsday postulating, and I had been told that this was harmful to my mental well-being as well as irrational. On some level I knew that what I imagined happening made no sense, but I hadn't been able to grip the irrationality of it until I met the word. *Catastrophize.* Because it was a word that the author had needed to use (perhaps coin), this tendency of mine must not be an isolated phenomenon. It must be common among persons like me, ergo, my paranoid fantasies might really be just that: fantasies. My spirits rose. I hung onto the word and waited to use it, monitoring my thoughts. *Catastrophize! You are catastrophizing again!* The existence of the word helped me diminish the syndrome it described. I'm sure someone versed in semiotics could explain why that should be so, and the explanation might have helped with my insomnia.

Around this time, I received an e-mail from my agent.

I'm very pleased to tell you that our British agents have placed Shiva 3000 with Pan Books ... I know you'll be pleased.

I stared at the news. *Don't start catastrophizing*, I thought. I patched together a reply that indicated enthusiasm.

Things that should have been comforts were concerns, accomplishments were crimes, good news was bad news. The inversions grew tiresome. The internet, too, had changed in my estimation. Instead of a revolutionary tool it had shown itself to be something less than healthy for me. *The Evolution of Useful Things* describes the surprising false starts along the way to the making of the fork, and reveals that canned foods were produced long before anyone had dreamed up the gadget to open them. It was a peculiar path to something even as simple as a Styrofoam cup. I had witnessed a tool's evolution before my admission to the ward. I had felt a change.

In the library, we had been connected to the internet before it became widely available to homes, but with just one terminal behind our reference desk in the central branch. The net then spread to librarians' desks in smaller branches, though at first I was more likely to use it than Gail. Next, public internet stations arrived, and we offered free training sessions to introduce the web to patrons. These were a big hit, curious Mennonites coming to add their names to the wait list, wanting to give this much-hyped thing a whirl. The library was a popular place for a while. Our number of public internet terminals doubled at about the same time that the demand for the service halved. Curious Mennonites now owned their own computers and had a cheap dial-up connection, and the people still using our stations were often shifty men who never bothered with books, or adolescent boys surfing for images of nipple-slips of female wrestlers. People who had regularly come to the library before the days of the internet seemed to come less often afterward.

During that first phase of library-internet evolution, the behind-the-reference-desk phase, a gangly, odd, verbose young man approached me. "I'm looking to do some historical research and I wondered if you could help me find some historical material because it's not an easy subject."

"Okay."

He went into a summary of events beginning in World War II, his knowledge already tiresomely detailed, connecting Bayer Pharmaceuticals to Nazi Germany and following the idea through to modern times, with alarming consequences for all, and though I hadn't heard this particular conspiracy theory before, I felt as sure of its dubious validity as I did of the whereabouts of information to please him.

I printed off six or seven pages from the web. He looked at the material in his hands as if I'd just given him the recipe for gold. "This is ... great!"

"But you should keep in mind —"

"It's all here, look at this!"

"Just remember —"

"This is going to make my research so much easier!"

"But —"

He spotted his younger sister, who couldn't find a book on toucans. "Ask this guy," he said loudly, pointing to me. "This guy rules!"

I shrank in my seat. What I had wanted to say was, "Bear in mind that you can't always trust information published on the web." We were occasionally reminded to say the same about information published in books, but internet stuff made the caveat so glaringly necessary that we should probably have invested in a rubber stamp so we could apply the phrase "Read with Caution" to printouts like the one I'd just handed over. But the moment had passed. It really had passed: soon internet stations stood throughout the library, without even a fidgety library employee to act as a buffer, and anyway the Bayer conspiracy guy was probably trying to figure out how he could get home access later that same afternoon.

When Michelle and I had been preparing for our trip to India, we had made an appointment with a physician who specialized in shots for travellers, as we wanted to be immunized against whatever exotic bugs might await. The specialist was a likable, jokey fellow who seemed really glad to be in his role. This was good, I thought, because Michelle was slightly nervous about tropical diseases we might encounter as well as the drugs to prevent them. She had begged time off work to do this, to drive out of town, almost all the way to Vancouver, to be here and receive the shots, then go back to work. The specialist was chatty, and I started to glance at my watch as he expounded about his role and the variety of dangers awaiting us. We were getting shots, a prescription and more shots later. Did we need a shot for Japanese encephalitis?

"That depends." He consulted his reference material. "Are you going to be near rural areas?"

"We're mostly going to large centres," I said.

"The medication is particularly recommended if you'll be travelling in rural areas."

"We'll be in places that visitors like to go to."

"No rural or swampy areas?"

"We might drive by a rural or swampy area, I'm not sure ..."

"You probably don't need this shot."

"Okay," I said. Good: it cost fifty bucks a pop.

"Still," he said.

"What?"

"It might be a good idea."

Michelle bit a nail. I sighed.

"Do we need to take it, really?"

"I know," he said, jogging happily to his desk. "Man, I love this." He referred either to his laptop or his internet connection. "I can get information that's up to date, up to the minute." We waited as he tapped at the keyboard, then his printer whirred with the sound of small rollers and the catch of blank sheets of paper. Soon he handed me a sheaf of pages.

"This is from a bulletin board I have access to with current information about diseases in Asia. It's all about disease, and some of the contributors are doctors out there, right in the field."

The swampy fields? There was a lot of material in the print-out. I could feel my temperature rising, even without tropical fever. We just wanted him to tell us: Did we need the shot or not? Didn't he understand that? Behind the easy grin and jokey manner, I sensed the concept of liability lingering in him, like an ailment of northern climes.

"I know what I'll do," he said, returning to the computer. "I'll send a query to the discussion board, ask those doctors directly. They can let us know their opinion of whether or not you need that shot."

"I don't think we have enough time to get their opinions," I said. "I'm sorry, but Michelle was supposed to be back at work fifteen minutes ago."

"No problem: you've still got enough time between your arrival date and when the drug takes effect."

Do we or do we not need this shot? I wanted to shout. He preferred not to say. He would rather defer to the internet. It was a mistake I too had made.

When we finally left his office and drove back to the valley, Michelle spoke, holding back tears. The appointment had done the opposite of what we had wanted for our confidence level. I dreaded making a decision about whether or not to take a shot for Japanese encephalitis.

There was no question we wanted to protect ourselves against malaria, and we did. What did that specialist say about Lariam? I can't remember. Given his manner, I can't imagine that he would not warn us against possible known side effects, or at least have given us a printout listing them, but it might have been buried in other warnings we received in the torrent of information. Michelle and I both took Lariam and worried about decisions that required no worry.

After I returned Michelle to work and went home, I booted up the computer and checked our e-mail, to find my inbox stuffed with messages from abroad, physicians from the subcontinent and beyond, weighing in virtually on the topic of Japanese encephalitis, did we need the shot, yes we did, no we didn't, it's been a slow year for Japanese encephalitis: you don't want to take any chances, maybe you should ... I could only gape and hit the delete button.

It's tempting to think of information overload as a syndrome in itself, that someone like Ruth perhaps absorbed one bit of trivia too much before passing out in her car and then entering the ward. But the people I knew who knew the most, like my brother Erik or my friend Carl, seemed untroubled by their huge knowledge. They seemed fortified by it.

What I perhaps felt around me at the time was how "knowing things" was changing and how the traffic in knowledge was shifting. Nowadays I see no point in memorizing the capitals of Europe or learning from someone how to hem pants, because I assume I can access that info on the web when I need it. It's an assumption that leaves me unfortified, but I accept it. Blessed with Google, I'll probably never need to ask Michelle's mother to teach me how to hem pants, definitely won't sign up for a night class to learn how to gap my plugs, can't see myself taking a book out of the library just to find out the capital of Belgium, but might, given my extra free time, marvel at how little resistance

I put up to the new convenience. I've surrendered certain forms of contact. I'm permitted to know so much less.

Years after my experience in the hospital, I found myself writing freelance articles for a small newspaper in Nova Scotia. I wrote one about an environmental protest that had been organized mostly through word-of-mouth and the web, and I relied on the organizers' website for much of my information. After the protest occurred, my editor asked me to write a follow-up, and when I rechecked that website, I gagged. In my first article I had reported that the organizers wished to remain anonymous; now I read: "Despite media reports to the contrary, we never were or wished to be anonymous," and the authors proceeded to take full credit for the protest. *I* had written that they wished to remain anonymous. *I* was that media about which they complained ... and I wondered if I was going nuts again, because I thought I'd read of their desire for anonymity on their site.

I felt like the horse in *Animal Farm*, going to the barn wall to recheck the rules. Then I discovered that I had saved that web page on my computer while writing the first article, and checking the saved version, I found that my recollection was correct. The authors had merely changed the content of their page, first requesting anonymity, then blaming the media for their anonymity. There was a medium to blame, all right, for this bit of Orwellian anxiety.

New anxiety accompanies new tools. In the Hotmail messages I had composed during my breakdown, I had placed information that felt, to me, momentous. After the e-mails were deleted, I couldn't stop fearing their existence. *Someone could still read them; my secret could still get out.* If a government agency wanted to discreetly copy e-correspondence or web pages, it would not be difficult to accomplish. The providers of Hotmail no doubt regularly back up the files on their servers — it's probably essential to the service, and there is no saying when, if ever, a message will truly be deleted. As much as I desperately wanted to destroy those e-mails, a message written on the web could never be swallowed, flushed down a toilet, torn into bits or obliterated by writing overtop in firm, looping strokes. You couldn't guess the path an e-mail would take to its destination, or guarantee that your words in that medium were anything but timeless.

Michelle felt the change, too. The web and e-mail were still novelties at the time of my admission, and using the computer didn't play to her strengths. While trying to access my Hotmail account for the first time with her retired minister friend sitting beside her, the two of them struggled away while the *Blade Runner* android tirelessly cursed them. "The internet," Michelle said recently, "was one more way I felt hopeless in the situation."

AT HOME, I re-established my access to the net. I wouldn't revisit the website that had so troubled me and led me to make plans for final exit, but I did remember how I had first found it, and could concentrate enough to do a search with Hotbot.

I had to find out. The possibility that a catastrophic series of events might roll off the publication of my novel lingered. I couldn't resist checking, just taking the pulse of the web, just a finger in the air to feel whether any storms brewed, somewhere, anywhere.

There was something different. I pursued a link to a news story. It concerned episodes of a popular television show featuring a leather-clad heroine, episodes not yet aired. In the script, the sword-wielding warrior woman encountered a demon of Hindu mythology and, in foiling him, teamed with the god Hanuman. A great cry of protest had arisen. The producers had tried to assure people that Hanuman was portrayed in the most sympathetic, evil-thwarting and favourable manner that their writers could conceive, but this had not assuaged the righteous critics, who had continued their complaint. Searching further, I found that the issue had already been resolved, and I swallowed dryly.

The producers had abandoned those episodes. They were yanked. The company had given up. Not good news. A bad sign. A terrible sign. A sulphurous, eerie wind.

I pushed back from the computer and felt my heart speeding. If a flattering portrayal of Hanuman could upset people, what would they make of my book? And if the producers of a hit television show chose to back off, well, what chance did I stand? Alone?

I got up. My ribs were a cage. I made my way to the kitchen and opened the cupboard. I grabbed the vial I wanted and shook out one of the tapered beige ovals, the one med I'd taken consistently since my admission to the unit and continued to take now: alprazolam, known better to the world by its trade name, Xanax.

Minutes after taking one, I could again sit in front of the computer and feel my fears crack, break up and float away, while parts of my body I couldn't place loosened. I looked at the screen. What had I worried about? Concerns wafted like broken cobwebs, drifting apart on a breeze.

My hospital charts recorded my anxiety level on any particular day with the ration of those pills, six tablets alprazolam, three tablets alprazolam. Out of the ward I took one daily with my anti-depressant and anti-psychotic, and another whenever anxiety hit. News about the TV show qualified. Within minutes it was a trifle.

I needed that pill earlier. When I was sixteen, maybe. It acted in my brain, enhancing some neurotransmitter, but where I felt it specifically was in that web of contradictory, problematic filaments that sometimes bound my body and other times made it tremble with perceived threats. With alprazolam, I can imagine boarding that plane to India, or cruising through an algebra final as I was meant to do, all the complex microscopic interactions of chemicals that ruled my body working themselves out, a long equation unravelling into a smoothly curved graph and releasing, without complaint, values of x and y. Had I, or somebody, recognized early on my character deficiency as an alprazolam deficiency, I might have stumbled across that anti-defamation website and seen such complainers only as variations of the kind of Christians who would protest a painting of a black woman at the Last Supper or object to Halloween decorations of witches in the library — not a group whose opinions I valued; in fact, I would have taken their scorn as a badge of accomplishment. If only! With alprazolam, I might have gotten through Lariam. Obsessive hand washing and Bell's palsy, getting overwrought about an algebra exam and getting nauseated reading Lewis Carroll, waking at the slightest sound or feeling woozy riding sideways on the bus — I suspected all of these things were symptomatic of a microscopic web within me, and that it cried out for a simple tonic delivered in a small, unglamorous, centre-marked-for-ease-of-cutting oval. It was a tool to deal with other tools. A palliative for an age. I wanted to take a small knife and carve a heart on the surface of a pill.

PERSONAL REVELATIONS

DOWN A FEW DOORS from the Day Program, closer to the ward but another notch away from it on the scale of mental fitness, the Depression Group met twice a week. Antoine and Joe didn't attend; I never saw either of them again.

This group was larger, maybe ten people, and looking around the circle, one could see different manifestations of depression in young and old, men and women. Actually, aside from one woman, everyone was under forty. A staff member I had met in the first program led the group, but the discussion here was different just for the fact these people actually participated. It had a whiff of Alcoholics Anonymous, but we began each session by stating how we felt, rather than how long we'd gone without drink. I was comfortable enough in the setting, but withheld details of my situation, especially about the book and being a writer. Was one of these people competent enough to use such information against me? Blackmail me somehow? Better to stay quiet.

The man I selected as the most obvious candidate for trouble was the second I had met with anger control problems. Whereas Antoine, when questioned, spoke with a gruff detachment that could be unsettling — especially when the cold had just darkened his glasses into shades and the subject was pointless revenge — Leon was animated, articulate. I could see anger problems in his tendency to finish whatever the facilitator started saying and to answer her questions with lengthy, information-packed replies. I didn't want to catch his attention. He would begin talking about something innocuous like back pain and segue into a rant about the furniture company that had formerly employed him, and soon he would rise from his seat, as if trying to stay at the same elevation as his voice, before he caught himself and put his fingers to the bridge of his nose, closed his eyes and counted to three.

He sat down, quieted but red-faced with residual fury. "Sorry," he said. "I'm sorry."

His knowledge of anti-depressants was exhaustive, especially the ones that had failed him. Our facilitator suggested a newer medication that had special promise in the area of anger control.

"I can't afford it," he said, looking down. Since losing his job, he had been reduced to delivering telephone books and picking up odd shifts at the waterslides. Over the course of a few sessions, he talked about his own shortcomings and spoke of them as openly as he did the things that incensed him. When he said he couldn't afford those drugs, I believed it: his depression had cost him his job and without his job he couldn't pay for a (possible) cure. My attitude toward him changed over a few weeks. I realized it on the day that Gary came to fill in for our absent facilitator, and I imagined Leon leaping from his seat to throttle Gary, my own fantasies of rage plausibly projected onto him. *We've heard that before! We know what our synapses look like! We're sick of John Cleese and his damn video!*

Leon, Bernard and other people who functioned well troubled me. If they could walk and talk and interact so comfortably, what were they doing here, in this place, *really*? It was a reliable anchor point for paranoid thoughts. But the benefit of a group like this, added to the fact that I was regaining perceptive abilities, was seeing the same people over a long enough period that I could realize they *weren't* functioning all that well, really, that they did come for a reason, with genuine problems and honest intentions. Of all the groups of people I'd been unwillingly plunged into, this bunch was the easiest not to distrust.

One of them was an eighteen-year-old named Julia whom I would have noted was gorgeous, had such an observation not been grossly out of place. She seemed glum when not doodling butterflies on her handouts, and I thought to myself, Why are you sad? Look at the rest of us! Maybe we could serve as a sort of shock therapy for her. Look at the bags under our eyes! The poor posture! Consider our questionable career choices, and those of us who have been abandoned by our partners, or snacked our way into near-obesity! You have nothing to be miserable about. Look at us, and avoid, avoid, avoid! But I knew you could get so low that even harsh evaluations of strangers couldn't lift your spirits.

Our group went for a stroll in the courtyard one afternoon. To get there, we needed to pass through the ward. I shuddered and hurried during the brief transition. I didn't really think the nurses would snap a plastic bracelet onto my wrist, but you could never be too certain, and there was nothing insane about a brisk pace. Outside, Julia walked alongside me.

"You're very sad, aren't you?" she said.

"Me? Well, I'm told I'm depressed."

"Sometimes I look at your face during group," she said, "and you look *so sad*."

I heard something unhitch in her throat with a quickening of breath, and now her shoulders rose; she brought a hand to her face and started to sob.

"I'm not that sad!" I said. "Really! Please, look at me, look at my face again. I'm smiling, see? Please, Julia, don't cry."

But she cried. And I suspected it wasn't my life or my look that upset her. She too projected.

Her despair deepened, and we saw it happen over the course of our meetings. I had found the word "catastrophizing" and felt somewhat improved, but she reported decreasing ability to face her schoolwork and graduation, and the very idea of her ex-boyfriend, for whose time and attention she still begged. "I was driving by the lake the other day," she told us. "You know where the road starts to really really turn? And I thought, it would be so easy. All I had to do was turn the steering wheel the other way, hard, and it would be over, I could imagine the car flying through the rail, into the water, going down …"

That silenced the group. The facilitator, too. We looked at one another. I'm not sure who put forward the idea of Julia spending time in the psych unit, immediately. She found the idea off-putting and bizarre at first but didn't reject it outright. Other group members started to speak positively of the ward and their experiences within — how right it had been for them at that particular nadir in their lives — hoping, obviously, that Julia might be persuaded to check herself in.

"And the food!" I said. "The food is really quite good. Yeah, I was impressed. It comes in these handy blue trays? You can pick what you want if you fill out these little sheets ahead of time. People always say hospital food is so bad but I found the opposite."

The others agreed, the food really was quite a highlight.

So much for letting the truth be my guide or whatever. I couldn't believe I was actually trying to sell the ward to someone. But there it was. And she did go in. "The food?" she said, afterward. "The food was awful. You guys totally lied about the food."

During a later meeting, the topic of employment came up as it was bound to, the facilitator wanting us to think about how we might sustain ourselves in the near future and work around our ailments and shortcomings. Julia was still in school, the elderly lady was retired, another woman was pregnant. Leon pondered buying a larger wagon for the release of next year's phone book. My turn came rapidly.

"I guess I'll keep working at the library," I said. "I don't know. Go back there ... maybe pick up more shifts ... maybe look at getting more education ... a degree in that ..."

Long pauses often went unfilled in the room, but this subject was more difficult for me to talk about than the others knew. Because I didn't know what I was going to do with my life. I'd never expected to face the question.

"I don't really want to do that ... it's not what I really want ..."

"What's the matter with library work?" the elderly woman asked. "I love the library!"

"It's just ..." I sighed.

The facilitator waited patiently, not looking at me.

"It's just that's not what I had *planned* to do, you know? It's not what I'd imagined doing with my life. The library is fine for a wage, but I had always thought I would accomplish something different, that I would manage to do just one special thing."

I spoke more quickly, and something in my tone woke the faces around me. Leon had put in a sympathetic *Yeah!* to the idea of doing something special with one's life and leaned forward in his seat. The facilitator turned to me and said softly, "But Jan. You have done something special. Something unique."

Again I sighed.

"Would you like to tell the group what it is that you've done?"

I confessed that I had written and sold a novel. They made sounds indicating that this impressed them.

"Yeah, but it's not that simple," I cut in. "I wrote this novel, but it's made problems for me. In fact it was the beginning of all my problems, what put me in the unit, what brought me here."

I explained. I went into details, gave a short version of my nightmare scenario. I wasn't going to catastrophize, after all — I would just explain as much as they needed to know to understand — but I was talking quickly, with unnecessary elaboration, and I had to rein it in before I found myself describing missile launches. I could and I would.

I shut up.

On the other side of the circle, Leon seemed agitated, alert, perhaps excited by my disclosure. "India?! Oh, they'll go nuts there. They'll rip you apart for something like that!"

I raised my eyebrows. He didn't seriously think that, did he? He was just trying to be polite, chime in, agree with me, right?

Anyway, I had said too much.

MY END-OF-THE-WORLD SCENARIO should have been more Hindu in flavour. That would have made sense, given my immersion in that material over the preceding years, and given that I felt I had breached Hindu sensibilities with my book. Hinduism could accommodate catastrophic visions. Why, during the worst of my delusions, had I not expected to see Vishnu riding forth on a white horse in his tenth and final avatar? I might have suspected we lived in Kali Yuga, a morally deficient era, and that the world approached the destructive end of that cycle, but mostly I had seen myself as an agent of a vaster religion, invisible yet obvious, to which all religious beliefs unknowingly belonged, and whose end-times were, in tone, distinctly Christian.

Since getting out of the ward, I had been accompanying Michelle to church on Sundays, something I had not done since childhood. The place was remarkably unchanged. Michelle had surprised me once by saying she thought it was a beautiful church, and I could see that now: there was something almost Scandinavian in the blond wood on view and the boat-like way the whole fit together. For the past fifteen years my view of this structure had been primarily from the exterior, as I drove by, and from this vantage it held little aesthetic appeal. Inside, the smell remained unchanged, too. How could a smell stay the same over such a long period? It wasn't a bad smell. But there was a smell.

Hanging high on the walls were felt banners I remembered from childhood. Each espoused some small bit of wisdom of the preachy variety, accompanied by a graphic image. Owing to the material, the pictures verged on cartoonish, felt being available in a limited palette and here cut in simple shapes to make the rendered object. The banner I remembered most vividly, and saw still hanging, featured a caterpillar on one side and a butterfly on the other, with a message in between reading: "*Who, me? Change?*" Perhaps the question that felt caterpillar should have been asking was, Who, me? Change the decorations?

But then again: Who, me? Change?

The minister had changed since my childhood days. I watched her manage the proceedings with about as much interest as I watched the wallaby's fibula being mended on *A Country Practice*. Stand up, sit down, greet your neighbour, please open your hymnbook and mouth the words to "Joyful, Joyful, We Adore Thee." Seated around me was the definition of decent people, and all but I put in an effort to try to make the proceedings pertinent and not dull, but I watched the sermons in a trance of indifference, for the most part, with the exception of one startling moment when the minister, listing a variety of scourges that plagued modern society, said, "Depression," and locked eyes with me. I shrank in my pew.

On one or two more occasions I saw Mr. Anderson, who did much to restore my perspectives simply by going on walks with me and chatting informally: topics could come up or not. I was interested to hear that in his training he'd been obliged to learn Greek to read the Bible in an early form. All of the details about the life of someone who had chosen this career I found interesting. I really hadn't imagined it before. He also said, on the subject of church attendance and participation, that men often decided that they wanted to return to the church and have it be a part of their life again, and that this usually happened when they turned thirty or thereabouts and found themselves husbands and parents. I recalled, from early on in my delusional state, one of my doctors telling me that young men often developed full-blown schizophrenia in their twenties. I was surprised to learn that a schedule existed for these things. I was twenty-nine. There was much expressed in that vintage banner, still hanging there, that metamorphosis in felt. It implied that the caterpillar had input in the decision to become a butterfly, but wasn't the truth more that it just sort of came upon the insect, unbidden, inescapable?

"Jan," Mr. Anderson said one afternoon, "I'm thinking about starting a men's group at the church. Something informal, meeting once a week. Would you be interested in joining such a group?"

"Sure!" I said.

But on my own, my throat tightened at the thought of it. I would have to explain myself at such a meeting, wouldn't I? My experience of this from group sessions was not positive. Was that me, even? Was I really someone who went to a men's group at the local church? My church? Someone who had a church?

I didn't go.

The idea of the first meeting decided it for me, the one where I would have to introduce myself and my background to men, real men, who had real jobs and families and couldn't relate to the experience of watching the world through the filter of an anti-psychotic drug or even the filter of being an aspiring writer. The best I could have managed by way of explanation was "I'm Michelle's husband," and hope that said enough. But chickening out was even easier.

And there would come a day in the spring, when my thirtieth birthday fast approached, when we got out of church and walked to the parking lot, and at the car I paused with my key in the lock, thinking, *phew*, now we can go have brunch, maybe go for a walk by the river, I can do some reading.

"You're smiling," Michelle said.

I said, "I think I'm starting to get better."

I STILL THINK OF THE MOMENT in K-Mart when we learned of the assault against Jacquie, and I pause before drawing any conclusions about religion, especially as practised in the Fraser

Valley. Because Jacquie had survived and gone on to become a professional and a mother, and she had done so, I learned, as a new member of one of those big churches around me, the kind I considered fundamentalist. Did her beliefs strengthen her? Fortify her? Years later she went to the prison where her brother was incarcerated and forgave him, and also went to the prison of the two other criminals, who had beaten her and her father with baseball bats as they slept in the hope of gaining money, and Jacquie forgave them, too. I don't know anyone who has gone through worse events, and the ability to function as a person and a professional seems like proof enough of strength, never mind the ability to face and forgive the people who could do such a thing to your life.

I didn't even feel inclined to forgive those people at that intersection downtown, the ones who stood waving signs at stopped cars. "Save your soul! Are you ready?" They considered themselves ready — *saved* — and Christian apocalypse seemed no disaster to them. To my mind it was a disaster, and an idea especially nightmarish during the brief phase in which it seemed imminent.

I had gotten it from people like that. Caught the idea like a cold, a mental flu, something I picked up on a doorknob and made my own, because I didn't properly wash my hands of it. Those people waving homemade signs on the corner hadn't meant to plant the seeds of nightmares. Such a thing had probably never occurred to them. But if they knew, would they mind? Perhaps if someone, in a dark hour of his or her life, recalled those signs outside the car window and because of them, came around to that way of thinking, that way of seeing the world, maybe the sign-bearers wouldn't mind seeming spooky. Maybe it would justify the effort, the insults, the jeers, the dozens of middle fingers. I wanted to ask.

But I couldn't find them. They didn't show up at their old haunt on the nights when I drove by, years later. I hardly recognized the intersection, so many storefronts had changed. I wasn't sure which of the churches in town might have produced the sign-wavers, so it was a lost cause.

But one sign remained — a big one. West of the dinosaur-themed attraction formerly known as Bedrock City and east of Chilliwack, on the last flat of the valley, toward where river met mountains and the highway bifurcated into twisting mountain passes, there the sign stood. *Prepare to Meet God.* But even slowing to 80 kmh, I found it difficult to tell which property the sign was on. Farmland. Houses and barns stood so far away it was a challenge to determine their position, and I took the next off-ramp and drove down roads to put me closer. But it was still hard. Now I was close to the homes but the sign was so far away I could hardly pick it out from billboards advertising the distance to the next McDonald's and "Dino-town." Big parcels of land. After I had done the circuit once more and decided on a house that seemed the likeliest, I pulled into the driveway and stopped the car. I looked around before getting out, as this was also dog bite country. I went to the door and rang the bell a few times. Maybe it was a dumb idea.

Nobody answered.

Even if I had the right property, the owners themselves probably had nothing to do with the sign. Who had put it up? *Prepare to Meet God.* I wanted to know what exactly that was supposed to mean.

Another question I longed to ask the billboard's sponsors and those people who stood on the street corner was how much consideration they had really given to the book called Revelation, to the words they waved in the air, and to the author. Had they ever thought of John of Patmos as a man, sitting somewhere on that island, writing? That maybe he had a point of view? Maybe he was angry and bitter about the circumstances of his day? That he might have been a regular ordinary man, in many ways, perhaps even someone who suffered from mental illness? Or maybe he was someone who suffered only from a vivid imagination, who had no other means of expressing himself, and didn't know when he had crossed a line.

LION BITES

DR. WHITMAN MOVED into a new office over the course of my appointments with him. I was glad to be removed from the hospital but had expected fancier digs. The spartan collection of furniture included no more than a battered filing cabinet or two, his desk and some chairs. To his credit, my psychiatrist had hung no free posters on the walls of his office.

"I got the letter from Harcourt today," I told him.

"Which letter was that?"

"About the book. They had someone look at it, and that person didn't find anything objectionable about it. So it's full steam ahead with the publication."

"And how do you feel about that?"

"I feel good," I said. "I feel good."

"It must have been reassuring to read that opinion of the novel."

"They had some qualms. Nothing major. So I guess I can go ahead and start looking forward to seeing the book in print."

"And how are your thoughts?"

"Better. I took an alprazolam when I got this news, but I'm fine."

"Are you still having concerns about reactions to your book?"

"Some. Nothing like before. No visions of doom."

We talked about other possible indicators of my mental health, and as usual it was a pleasant chat. Dr. Whitman, like Gail, had a gift for putting people at ease and making them feel comfortable talking, or at least for me he did. Partly it was the casualness of our conversation, as he would tell me about his upcoming vacation plans or leisurely pursuits.

"Ever read any Patrick O'Brian?" he asked one day.

"No."

"Wonderful author. His books are set during the Napoleonic wars, but touch on many fascinating topics. The ship's surgeon is also a naturalist, you see, and as they travel the globe, he investigates natural phenomena. You wonder how a writer like O'Brian can be so knowledgeable in such a broad range of subjects — all of that historical detail."

"Hm."

I had no direct knowledge of Patrick O'Brian. I'd drawn an opinion of him as I had of Wodehouse, solely from the books' covers, which seemed deliberately similar. And as with my brother and the Wodehouse book, I felt the surprise of learning what someone reads for pleasure.

When we had run out of things to say, the psychiatrist scheduled my next appointment, and with my increasing mental stability, the length of time between visits grew.

As part of my return to life, I went back to work. "I just told people you were sick," Gail stage-whispered to me before my first shift began. I didn't find the setting as difficult as expected, but concentrating on even simple tasks was hard. I felt as if I were operating from within a fog. But I went through the motions, and the motions were pretty much the sum of my responsibilities, particularly the motion of a wand across a barcode. No patrons from my last night here came in; the nurse who'd bolted from the internet station never returned. I hoped she hadn't complained to Somebody Higher Up in the chain of command. It was all such a stupid waste. Our page arrived at his regularly scheduled hour, and when it was just he and I, I tried to apologize for that evening.

"I was mentally ill," I said stiffly.

"That's ohh kayyyy," he said with a smile, sounding out the syllables in a pleasant, singsong way that suggested my problems ran very deep indeed.

Mr. Anderson had encouraged me to be forthright with people about what had happened, but among the difficulties this presented was word choice. When I returned to the library's headquarters for a shift, the head of the department where I was assigned called me into her office, the same woman who had offered me a place within her miracle-cloth-selling empire. I had been out of commission for a long time, and what I wanted to tell people, if I was going to be honest about things, was that I had gone crazy. "Mentally ill" seemed too vague; sometimes it sounded as innocuous as a bad headache and in other conver- sations it seemed to leave open the possibilities of cannibalism and fecal antics. Crazy is what I had been. Temporarily crazy but crazy, nonetheless. I would understand if other people with similar problems disliked or even feared that label, but I had struggled to find a word to match the experience I had just gone through and only "crazy" seemed to do it. I had been alive and I had perceived the world around me, but it was reflected within me in a faulty manner, as one might expect of a crazed mirror, breaking up at the fissures, the breaks following unpredictable routes, the whole not coming together to make a representative picture.

"Jan!" she said. "So good to see you! I heard that you were sick."

"Yes."

"I knew you were getting sick, I could see it. You were getting *so thin*. How long were you in hospital?"

"About three weeks."

"Three weeks! What was the matter with you?"

"I was in the psych ward," I said. I tapped my head. "A nervous breakdown."

"Oh," she said. "Oh." The smile left her face. It was hard to know how to respond to that revelation, I could understand, and I felt sullied having used the expression "nervous breakdown," a phrase I found small and antiquated and, worst of all, pathetic. It made the afflicted sound so ... helpless. It implied a larger inability to deal with life. Maybe I disliked the term because it was too apt. Feared that it was. But "I went crazy" was unlikely to make for a more comfortable conversation, and I simply left her doorway and went to the small office where I was assigned, without saying any more.

At home I tried to resume the central occupation of my life. While in the ward, I'd vowed never to return to writing. I saw it as an obvious part of my problem, part of what had sent me there, and lacking value. It didn't improve the world in any way — not my fiction, at least. In fact, close examination of my desire to be a writer would reveal nothing but character flaws — a desire for fame, fortune and renown as someone gifted with words. It was an egocentric pursuit that put added pressure on my spouse due to its meagre and scattershot pay. It was not good. Self-indulgent. I didn't consider it a worthy indulgence and wanted to be better.

But what else would I do? Writing was the one thing I had real training in, the one thing I felt any appetite for, and I had invested much time and toil in getting to my current level. I would be a published novelist within a couple of months. Squandering all that effort also seemed wrong.

I would write for the purposes of good, then. I would be a moralist: a C. S. Lewis for current times. Yes! That was what the world needed. I had loved those Narnia books as a child, and if Lewis could do it, why couldn't I? Why couldn't I write fantastical books that carried an undercurrent of moral instruction? Deliver some good into the world in an entertaining fashion, no doubt with my own oversized lion recurring in plotlines to gently nip off the heads of evildoers. That was it!

If I had pitched this solution to my caregivers, they might have viewed it as continued evidence of grandiosity, but for my part I saw it as the perfect solution to both my crisis and my skills.

For Christmas that year I received from my sister-in-law a boxed set of the Narnia books, a series I hadn't looked at since devouring it whole in elementary school. At the time I had been oblivious to the elements of Christian allegory — the Lion dying and being reborn a few days later had struck me as nothing more than an exciting and unexpected plot twist — and had I been forewarned, I probably would have given the books a wide berth. I tried them again now: this was among the first fiction I could process from start to finish. But, like many childhood passions, the Narnia books just didn't hold up to my pleasant memories of them. Some books could only be appreciated at the right age, and past that phase they had little impact. A wardrobe no longer seemed a credible portal to another world. I felt a misplaced sympathy toward the ice queen and could imagine being attracted to her, given the right circumstances. No, I was no C. S. Lewis for the upcoming millennium, but the boxed set was handsome, with tasteful illustrations on three sides, and I found the right spot to display it on my bookshelf as a souvenir of places I had gone in my reading but could not return to.

It also reminded me that books with an obvious moral purpose repelled me. They didn't work, because most people, thinking people, sniffed out teaching moments and found them off-putting. No, the best I could do was try to be honest in my writing — true, somehow — and let people draw conclusions on their own. I could still try to write in an entertaining fashion. There was nothing wrong with entertainment; people didn't read to be bored, after all. Except under unusual circumstances.

So, with a few steps of rationalization, I had gone from vowing never again to sit at my computer, back to what amounted to my old style of writing.

But. I didn't. Couldn't.

I sat, facing the white screen. I would write a line or two. I'd felt writer's block before, but only with sections of stories that didn't work or limp endings. Never before had the question been: What can I write about? I usually had a hard time picking between ideas. I tried switching from the computer to my pen and clipboard, but that was no help.

A monkey. A monkey with purple fur and sharp little teeth. And he owns a pistol. Perhaps he carries it on his back in a specially made holster. And this pistol, it's the last gun in the world.

I could see that this was a brilliant premise brimming with narrative potential, yet what happened to the monkey? Nothing. He was just another well-armed primate. I envisioned a purple squirrel monkey. Perhaps someone would remark on his unusual colour, in his presence.

"You think people are colour-coded for your convenience?"
he replied. "So you can tell who is bad and who is good? Well,
let me tell you that that is a very old and very dangerous
misconception."

Profound, profound. Yet it never amounted to more than a remark in a void, echoing in the white space beneath it. To whom did he say this? What was the context? After an hour or so I had produced nothing like an answer to these questions, not even an interim answer, not even an attempt at a resolution or a larger setting. In similar circumstances before, I had with good results gone to my Big Book of Ideas, which contained many loose notes and story ideas, and I now flipped through the various sections, adding characters and details to a list of things that might work in a story about a gun-owning monkey.

- Square mountains.
- A pregnant woman who couldn't give birth.
- People addicted to a kind of sugar, a sweetness they remembered from childhood but couldn't find.

When I had done this before, I would look for a connection between the listed elements, bring them together, see what happened.

- A librarian who sought certain overdue books, under
  contract ...

Today the ideas formed nothing more than a list. I did write:
I put words down, maybe a page and a half, but already I had
spent the ideas and sparked no new ones. The next day I tried
again, and the next day, and it was the same.

"I think it's the anti-psychotic," I told Dr. Whitman at my next
appointment.

"You do?"

"If it suppresses deluded thoughts, couldn't it also suppress
creative ones?"

"Hmm ..." He didn't like to be pinned down on that kind of
thing.

"I just find myself sitting there trying to generate ideas, and
nothing comes. Nothing. I've never been like this before. That
part of me feels ... inert. And I think that a drug that works on the
brain the way my anti-psychotic does probably has other effects,
including on creativity."

"But you're on such a small dose now," he said reasonably.

I sighed. It wasn't the answer I'd hoped for. I wanted him to
tell me I could drop that med, but he'd laid out a rough timetable
for taking me off it and the other two — alprazolam and doxepin
— and it appeared that we would be sticking to that schedule.
I would be weaned.

I wanted to blame the drug. If I couldn't, then I was the
problem. What if I had come out of the ward having lost even
the dubious asset of creative thought? I found I would say things
like, "Did you let the dog out?" The other person would look at
me funny, and inform me: "You just said, 'Did you let the *doorknob*

out?'" And I would wonder if I had really said that, I would examine the afterimage of the statement lingering in my head, give the sentence a quick mental palpation for its component words before it fully evaporated. Maybe I *had* said "doorknob." And I suppose I had made that kind of stupid substitution before this experience, but not as frequently, and it has stayed with me since. To me this suggests that my brain was partly rewired during descent or recovery, and I worried that the loss of creativity was another example of the restructuring. I much preferred to be like one of Oliver Sacks' patients in *The Man Who Mistook His Wife for a Hat*, Witty Ticcy Ray, a Tourette's sufferer who found that, yes, a course of Haldol kept him from bursting out in expletives, but also, on the drug, he was cast from good parts of himself: the genius jazz drummer, the person who enjoyed jumping in and out of revolving doors, the old self, whom he missed. Well, writing was my revolving door and I didn't want to just go around and around like this. I wanted the leaps back, my imaginative leaps, and I felt unwilling to trade them for a medication I probably didn't need any more.

I had never been comfortable linking creativity to madness. There was a changeover, sometime after Virginia Woolf filled her pockets with stones and waded into deep water, when madness came to be seen as an authorly gift, even a prerequisite, allowing the sufferer to see things that the hoi polloi could not, like bees seeing colours in flowers beyond our spectrum, miniature runways into deeper caches of pollen. I didn't like to hear authors use madness as a badge of authenticity, but I had a vivid memory of the connection.

I had been writing stories for years before entering university, but only there, in third year, did I experience what other writers described as "a story writing itself." Of course, stories never write themselves, but the feeling was a weird and distinct one, of having a sudden rush of ideas come together and fill out page after page, seemingly unbidden, new ideas emerging easily, perfectly, and producing what was a much better narrative than you could have expected. In a book called *Touched with Fire*, Kay Jamison describes the phenomenon broadly as "mental fluency." At the time, it had felt to me like a loosening of the brain, letting things flow that were otherwise restrained, and I remember then comparing the sensation — favourably — to going crazy. It was a good kind of crazy, a kind that wanted accompaniment by laughter, a giddiness, all the connections you didn't know you could make. It was a funny conversation around a table where everyone keeps adding to and elaborating on a joke.

In the ward, staring at the courtyard, I had felt the same process, an uncontrollable tendency to make connections. If I spotted someone in coveralls, he was an undercover agent waiting for his moment. If the cable cut out, it was because he had tried to cut the power before breaking in. If a nurse told me to go to my room, it was because the staff wanted my abduction to be accomplished in private. Everything fit. It was the flip side of my prof learning how to climb mountains for a story: he sought telling details that would lend his story authenticity, but in my ward mindset, mundane details around me proved the authenticity of my delusion. Paranoia is probably an evolutionary leftover, a tendency to hear a branch break in the night and wonder what stalked you, but to me in the ward, it was story making. Instead of creating a plot, I imagined plots against me. I could feel bad things about to happen when I learned of my roommate's new rubber sheets — it was foreshadowing. This was something you felt when reading, something you practised feeling when reading.

The feverish analysis I had done trying to determine the true identity of my first psychiatrist resembled my way of writing characters, too. I knew one or two details about him, plus things I inferred from what he said — his choice of tie, his haircut, his nephew's example — and the result was a kind, educated man who happened to be a Christian, doing his best to treat a difficult case. Or! He was a law-and-order type, a fundamentalist who felt the downfall of society so acutely that he was willing to bend confidentiality rules to inform the RCMP when a truly dangerous individual came to his attention. Small details were like stones in the stream of my thoughts, and I went with the flow, wherever the flow might lead. It was an unhinged way of thinking.

Boy, did I miss it! Or at least, some of it. I wanted back the portion that was my lone, dubious talent.

An armed monkey needed conflict, perhaps. Yes, an antagonist or antagonists. What type of people might cause trouble for a monkey who carried a gun? Perhaps the gun was coveted. Maybe it was a MacGuffin. If it was the last known gun in existence, possibly hunters sought it. Collectors. Assassins. "But the most dangerous group of all," I wrote, "was cowards. It is the ideal weapon of a coward."

The line sat, did not multiply. It sat as inertly as me in my chair. Maybe a monkey possessing the last gun in the world was in fact a stupid idea, but that had never stopped me before. "He used the word 'monkey' a lot to describe himself and I slowly realized it wasn't merely a simplification, but a euphemism he liked to encourage in the view others had of him."

I complained to Dr. Whitman.

"I sit there for half a day and that's the best I can do. One or two paragraphs and nothing more."

"You're worried about that?"

"A little."

He seemed sympathetic but I had not succeeded in bringing the topic around to my course of the anti-psychotic and a hastier conclusion to it.

"The newest Patrick O'Brian novel was just published," he said.

Again with Patrick O'Brian? Didn't he remember we'd had this conversation? "Oh yeah, I think I saw a review of it somewhere or other."

"I've already bought my copy," he said. "Such a knowledgeable writer. One wonders how he can do it, write in a voice appropriate to that time period, and with such detail and precision."

"Hm."

He seldom gave advice on how I might profitably change my life, but later in the conversation, he said, "Maybe you shouldn't read so much science fiction."

I probably nodded my head and smiled, but I felt saddened. Maybe the doctor and I weren't as good friends as I'd believed.

I didn't read a lot of science fiction any more. Yes, at the beginning of my university days I had had a T-shirt specially printed with the cover image of an awful horror novel I had recently enjoyed (*The Nightrunners* by Joe Lansdale), and wore it to my first creative writing class to declare my loyalties. But nobody in that class seemed to take umbrage (or notice). It was flimsy protection against new ideas, anyway, as I emerged from university aware of more kinds of fiction, and with my enthusiasm for Stephen King novels and sf rejigged, squeezed into a smaller amount of reading space. I knew of authors doing great things within genre fiction, but for me the labels seemed to limit more than they permitted. Part of what had pleased me about Harcourt buying my novel was that they intended to publish it like any other fiction title, with no possibility of bosomy women in form-fitting space garb appearing on the cover. Didn't Dr. Whitman appreciate this?

Patrick O'Brian. The series seemed to be something the psychiatrist, in his subtle way, wanted to prescribe to me. Maybe he thought it wasn't too far from my current tastes, but healthier. It had that escapist element, and it entertained with plot and exposition alternately. When I finally listened to the audiobooks, I wondered if Whitman realized just how close the series *was* to science fiction. The O'Brian books featured Jack Aubrey, the lusty ship's captain and central character partnered to Maturin, the level-headed doctor and naturalist, and the two of them seemed easily swapped for Kirk and Spock, travelling aboard their ship to exotic new lands, dealing with the crew and encountering familiar enemies along the way: nineteenth-century *Star Trek*.

My other problem with the psychiatrist's opinion of science fiction was that it seemed simplistic, almost clichéd. It reminded me of advice I'd overheard him giving Rodney, to avoid staring too long at his computer monitor with its flashing lights. Silly, really.

On the other hand. Science fiction was different from other fiction, and in the hands of a skilled author, it could be potent. Oliver Morton, writing in *The New Yorker*, articulated this difference well in his review of a Michael Crichton novel, *Prey*. Morton drew attention to the way the story and central crisis end:

This kind of resolution, too, is something of a Crichton trademark. He's forever describing things that could change the world — but don't ... The fact that Crichton has no interest in showing what might have happened is what makes him a writer of suspense fiction, rather than science fiction. A science fiction writer would naturally want to see what would happen if the technologies stayed out of control (as most do), and might even want to ask whether the consequences would be all bad (as they often aren't) ... *Prey*, with its kill-them-all-and-get-out approach, is neither as frightening nor as fascinating as Greg Bear's novelette of twenty years ago, "Blood Music," in which the characters, transformed by the nanotechnology within them, become both far more and much less than human.

In the novel *Blood Music*, Bear recycles that story and follows its premise further and, as Morton describes, with no looking back. A book that starts out as an effective techno-mystery becomes surreal, chilling, and exhilarating. Apocalyptic. In science fiction, a person or the world can be transformed, irreversibly, and I could recognize that as an element bleeding over from speculative novels I admired to my nightmarish visions for the outcome of my first major publication. Maybe that was the reasoning behind my psychiatrist's advice — not that science fiction caused mental illness or delusions, but if they should strike a person, he or she became vulnerable to familiar narratives.

O'Brian's Aubrey/Maturin series would not end with Napoleon crowned king of England; you didn't need to finish the series to know that. The books would stay within boundaries. It was a covenant swiftly established, by prose style alone; it was partly established by those similar covers. And if you happened to go crazy under the influence of Patrick O'Brian, maybe you could expect more palatable delusions than mine had been, as well as a quicker recovery. My roommate Rodney struck me as someone who had lost control while under the influence of his gilt-edged, leather-cased King James. I also learned of a friend's experience, a woman of a certain generation and an Elvis fan. She too had a breakdown, and in her imbalanced state, she did what the song "I Want You with Me" suggested she do: she climbed the mountain and prepared to swim the ocean, waiting for another Elvis fan, her ex-husband, to return. If you entered a situation where your mind was loosened, if you went adrift with it and found yourself reaching for a familiar story, which would be within reach?

THE THOUSAND NATURAL SHOCKS

WHILE STILL YOUNG enough for my mother to read me bedtime stories, I picked up the novelization of *Star Wars*. I begged her to read from this instead of another tale from the Danish Aesop's Fables, and she did give it a try, but the description of the rebel soldier's eyes bulging out as he was strangled proved more than she could stomach.

"Ugh," she said. "I think you're going to have to read this one yourself."

Here the being-read-to-sleep part of our relationship ended, and our reading tastes veered apart. Irreversibly apart, as it turned out, because she died before mine had the chance to swing back.

After my brothers and I sold the house and I spent a lot of time clearing out old crap, I found a book on the shelf that I had previously only noticed for the colour of its spine. It was *If On a Winter's Night a Traveller* by Italo Calvino, a book I had read in university, and I could imagine that had she lived long enough, I might have phoned home and spoken to my mother about books on my reading list, and I might have mentioned this one for the extravagance of its title, and she might have said, "Oh, Calvino! I've read that ..." and a conversation might have ensued.

But it didn't happen. I knew it was my mother's book; my father read non-fiction, primarily *The Vancouver Sun*.

My mother was the one who had gone to the library, and when I found myself back in the acquaintance of Gail the librarian, I had an unexpected source of memories of my mother. Gail said she remembered that my mother was friends with another patron whom Gail considered a snob, and I wondered if this was Gail's way of telling me, without putting it too bluntly, that she thought my mother was a snob, too. But if the snobbery showed up in choice of books (and friends) in a small rural library, I was okay with it. I was more than okay with it.

In the ward, I had sometimes felt a sense of déjà vu, that I had already seen this place, that I remembered the general layout of the lounge. Maybe, I first thought, I confused memory with a fragment of a dream. Dreams could be tricky, even when God wasn't using them to pull your leg. But I had been here before.

One day, when I was seven or eight, my brother Erik and I came home to find the front door locked. This was strange but not a problem; we went around to the side of the house where his room was, where we knew that an old window could be pushed up from outside and we could pull ourselves into the house.

The stranger thing was that our mother was in that room, Erik's room, sleeping on his bed. An odd thing to find, but maybe she had felt tired here. She was a nurse and sometimes worked nights, and we were accustomed to her sleeping during the day. I don't know if Erik, six years older than me, found the discovery more alarming than I did; I've never asked him. All I knew at the time was that she slept very soundly, because I tried my best to "accidentally" wake her. I had important news. We were learning to read in school, and as we progressed, we left behind our first readers and took up new ones. I was holding my first new reader and knew my mother would be as pleased as I was. But she dozed. I prodded her discreetly, and still she slept. Feeling certain that my new reader would be the first thing she would want to see upon waking, I stood it on my brother's bedside table, slightly opened so that the cover kept it upright, and she could see Dick and Jane or whoever upon opening her eyes. But she kept sleeping. She slept, and eventually my father came home, and she slept, and eventually an ambulance came, and she slept, as attendants moved her onto a gurney, rolling it through the house and loading her into the vehicle, sleeping all the while.

Shortly afterward, my class visited the hospital to sing for seniors. I had asked if, since we were going to be in the hospital, I could also visit my mother, who was a patient. This happened: my teacher took me away from the rest of the class and I went down for my first visit to the psych ward. I remember the place, but I don't remember the visit with my mother. I prefer to think it was a happy one for both of us.

If I wrote a piece of fiction about a writer who went crazy during the approach of his novel's publication and tried to kill himself with an overdose of sleeping pills, I might be tempted to include a flashback, toward the end, where he remembered from childhood his mother's suicide attempt. But I would use caution with that kind of thing. It's just too handy — acceptable, maybe, in a story for a second-year creative writing workshop — but even in that setting probably too convenient an insight into the main character's character. The detail about the new school reader would put it over the top.

Why she took the overdose, I never knew. It became an unspoken episode in our household and almost slipped from memory altogether. She was a nurse, which, I think, was part of it. Being a nurse was hard; I had made life hard for some! I could imagine a toll on the psyche, on a nurse's defences, being faced with an unending string of patients, of neediness, walking through colour-coded hallways and the ever-present smell of pee. Being a psych patient in your own hospital must also have been hard.

Some time later, Erik put up that poster I remember from his room, a photo of a skier coming down a slope, fast, accompanied by the slogan, "A Sound Mind in a Sound Body." Was it a reminder to himself? Or to blue parents who might wander into his bedroom? Years later he would go to Cambridge for his Ph.D. in physics. A sound body and a sound mind — he had both. Though we all shared a percentage of genes, my mother and I, for some reason, had neither.

During one of my mother's stays in the unit, I went to Saltspring Island to spend time with her aunt, Hedvig. It was a good time, apart from me occasionally waking in the night with a shock — sudden, intense knowledge that my mother was in the hospital. When, as an adult, I emerged from the unit and had to tell this same great-aunt where I had been, the conversation was awkward. How could I say it? She was almost ninety. I groped for a euphemism.

"I wasn't physically sick."

"Oh?"

"I was in the psych ward. I —"

"Was it your nerves?" she said.

Yes, I said, my nerves. Hedvig had once been a nurse too, and that word came like a diagnosis from an earlier era — one word, as broad an explanation and as easily tossed out as "genes" is today. "Nerves" still carried weight. She had hit a nerve. I was a nervous wreck for a while there. It had been a nerve-wracking time for all.

She told me once that somewhere in our family tree perched Soren Kierkegaard, though other relatives cast doubt on this idea. Kierkegaard seems as well known for mental unrest as for his ideas about existence and personal choice. They crossed into each other. And what about Hans Christian Andersen? He has been described as bipolar, and it says something about conflicted personality that a man who disliked children should choose to write fairy tales for them. I wondered about Hamlet. An icon of self-doubt and inner torment, suffering the slings and arrows; a character in a play, a figment of a literary imagination, but I couldn't help but wonder why Shakespeare had made him a *Danish* prince. Had Shakespeare met a Dane who suggested this origin was appropriate to a tormented soul?

Michelle and I visited Denmark for the first time as a couple. It was my first time back since I was twelve. It was a different place to me at thirty-one, and the frequent picturesque vistas struck us. I was pleased to think I had roots in a country where one might admire the beautiful shape of a building and realize that it was a parking garage. I felt I could somehow take credit for all of this. Often, as we travelled the country, we would see the familiar white shape of another church, beautifully preserved but poorly attended, its facade stepped, shaped like two matching flights of stairs leading up to the same blue sky.

Inside one of those churches, passing beneath the model boat suspended from the ceiling, my uncle explained his reasons for no longer attending regularly. "When a friend or neighbour dies, we go to church. For the funeral. Then, I find I don't need to go again so soon to church."

Cases of bad nerves appeared on my mother's side of the family with regularity. Sad nurses and doctors appeared in my family tree, as well as melancholic Lutheran ministers who inflicted their temperament on others long before the days of anti-depressants. I had an uncle who suffered severe, recurring bouts of depression and found relief only in electroconvulsive therapy. But the person whom my great-aunt associated most often with the problem of nerves was my mother's younger sister.

As a twelve-year-old, I had felt apprehensive about meeting my aunt Sif, having built up an unpleasant image of what someone suffering from "nerves" might be like, but I found then, as I did during our later trip, that she was a sweet woman — quite happy, mostly, and easy to be around. She did have a unique, bird-like manner. She might wander about the back yard, leaning forward slightly as she moved without direction or specific goal, getting behind a rose bush or stopping at a random point on the lawn. When her husband took us sightseeing on a broiling summer day, she didn't get out of the car, preferring to sit inside, bundled in her big wool coat and gloves while we enjoyed the scenery. Her laughter suggested tears were an equal possibility; there was always a moment when her changing expression hinted at more emotion being let loose than the situation merited — emotion unconnected to the situation, maybe. But she was nice. Despite the distress nerves had caused in her life, she had mothered a child.

"Michelle," she asked, in her troubled way, "why do you think Karoline became a nun?"

Having never met my cousin Karoline, and having just met Sif an hour earlier, Michelle might have been forgiven for not having an answer. It was a question people on this side of my family often asked. I hadn't seen Karoline since that first trip, when she had been a highlight, an older cousin willing to teach me how to play poker and paddle me in a canoe through bulrushes on a hot summer afternoon. I wouldn't have predicted a future for her in a convent. Who could have? Sif and her husband were not particularly religious. They certainly weren't Catholics. Most of the country was Lutheran and showed declining interest in religion. Michelle couldn't say why my cousin Karoline had chosen to become a nun. It had happened to her as a young woman. It seemed like a question that Sif had probably asked herself every day since. There was no satisfying answer to offer her.

THE PURPLE MONKEY produced no story. Nothing! I expected him to say things, make puzzling observations about the animal kingdom and mankind, but he remained mute, and surrounding him with scrap dealers, pharmacists or librarians made no difference. The story would not start, and I could only stare at the blank white representation of a page, wondering if my monitor strobed its light into my eyes at so high a frequency I couldn't see it happening or notice the effect on me.

I thought about my doomsday scenario.

I could almost see it working in a bad, end-of-the-world-style thriller novel. As a plot device it was almost plausible enough to work, a writer going into a psych unit because of his book, and then the book creating havoc around the world, leading to the possibility of war.

But the story would be better, I thought, if things weren't revealed in that order. And if it was told from the point of view of a character other than the author. In that version, the book would cause controversy and lead to international tensions, and the author would repeatedly tell interviewers that he had had no inkling of the conflict that his work would cause, and that he thought it ridiculous, really, and unfortunate. Then a reporter from a small local newspaper would dig deeper, perhaps acting on a tip from a nurse, and discover that the author had actually gone into the psych ward prior to the book's publication, predicting this very series of events, and the reporter would learn it all and let the world know of his visions of nuclear conflict, apocalypse along religious lines, et cetera, and populations would get into a real froth as a result.

Yeah, that would work better. That could be really freaky.

I picked up the draft of a novelette I'd worked on prior to my admission. It told the story of David and Goliath but from Goliath's perspective, following him from childhood to the moment when the stone struck. I had thought it would be fun to write a story in which the reader knew where the plot must go and how those events would someday form a Bible story, all the while seeing it from the point of view of the Philistine, who didn't have a clue, of course, wouldn't attach any significance to the identity of David, beyond the fact that he was a child. It would be about point of view, I thought.

I liked the story, but it lacked ... what? In my research I had stumbled upon a notion that perhaps David hadn't slain Goliath, really, that even in the Bible the killing was attributed to another Israelite. That could provide an interesting bit of ambiguity and add a layer to my story. But how would Goliath know about such a thing? If he died on the field, and the story was told from his point of view, how would he ever learn of this?

Maybe he fell but didn't die. The stone knocked him out but didn't kill him. How could a stone kill a giant, anyway? Maybe the head had been taken from someone else. And Goliath would wake, and learn his own story.

It felt, in my mind, as if a dam had been breached, a great synapse awakened, the leaps like a wash of neurotransmitters suddenly filling a great, dry gorge.

And what if Goliath kept waking? In different historical eras? What if he couldn't die, and kept arising all through time to hear his story again and again?

"Eventually he hears it incorporated into the Bible and finds he's portrayed as an enemy," I told Dr. Whitman at one of our last meetings. "He didn't think of himself as the bad guy."

"I see."

"Eventually he hears the word 'philistine,' and now it's a word used to describe not his people but someone who's just stupid, uncultured."

"But Jan."

"Because he keeps living, he's around long enough to see his own story and his own name get swept up and carried away by language and reading."

"I understand. However —"

"Maybe he sees the evolution of weapons, too, from David's sling and stone to cannons, to ... well, I've only got an outline."

At last I could report to the psychiatrist that writing was going well. Very well. Better than ever! But I could see from his smile that he waited to say something.

"Do you think it's wise?" he said.

"What?"

"Religious subject matter? Remember, how people might receive your novel, that was your main concern when you entered the unit."

I hadn't thought of that.

"I don't think it'll be a problem," I said.

AWKWARD PARTIES

THE IDEA OF A WRITER receiving a box of copies of his own novel
and taking out one to marvel in surprise at the look of it was, I
found, a cliché that didn't quite match reality. When my heavy
box came, I did anxiously rip it open to examine a copy, but I had
seen the book emerge beforehand. I knew what the layout looked
like, the type, I had received a cover and knew weeks before how
the blurbs and flaps would read. I did want to refamiliarize myself
with the dedication and look at the brief preamble that was the
one artifact of this period in my life. The true part of the cliché
was the sensation of holding your book for the first time, sliding
off the dust jacket to see the title embossed on the spine, flipping
through clothbound pages. The virtual made real. Months later,
my editor materialized, too. I had searched for and found a picture of him on the web before our meeting, so I would have a
sense of what he looked like. But suddenly, seated across from me,
was the personality that had come through in our e-mail corre-
spondence, and it was a relief to see a person attached to it. "All
writers are crazy," he said over dinner with a chuckle, and that
was the total of the references he made to my difficulties.

I considered giving Dr. Whitman a signed copy of the novel,

but I wasn't sure. It didn't feel quite like a celebratory thing to do, like an appropriate expression of thanks. First, I didn't really think he would enjoy it. I was no Patrick O'Brian, after all. It stung to imagine my psychiatrist reading the prologue, or just the title of the prologue, before gently closing the book and placing it on a shelf to prop up other books he would never read. Or worse, perhaps he'd toss it on top of a picture I'd seen in his office, presumably the work of another patient, a harsh welter of pen-and-ink lines filling a sheet to form a leering, humanoid figure.

A thank-you card it was.

"I really appreciate everything you did for me," I said to him. "You made a huge difference."

"Well," he said, "I'm just glad your recovery was so routine."

Routine? It wasn't the word I would have chosen.

My breakdown had marred the publication, at least for me. I hadn't expected that the first place where people knew me not merely as friend or relative or library employee, but as a writer, would be a hospital psych ward. It was not what I expected, any of it. Months had passed since my discharge, and I could convince myself I felt okay now, depression and delusions and psychotic thinking behind me, and that I was proud to see the book in print, but I couldn't separate one from the other, they remained twined. Friends and family knew the connection. Was it the most awkward congratulations party in history, the one Michelle threw in our apartment upon the book's release? Or did a more awkward moment occur at the party Gail organized at the library, the modest turnout of well-wishers including, most chattily, a woman who wanted my help breaking into the Christian fiction marketplace? Now she knew where to find me.

Time passed. My friend Carl, the physician, moved his family south of the border, the brain drain in action. K-Mart went bankrupt and Wal-Mart filled the void. In Safeway, auto-sprinklers were installed in the produce section. Once, I had walked through a similar produce section with a detachable rubber hose and manually sprayed the veggies as required, deciding how much a head of lettuce should drip. Time dripped on. Hands of the giant Safeway clock moved.

I came to understand that my book would not set the world afire. It didn't even earn out its advance! After I got a few embarrassing royalty statements, the fact that my novel had not been the catalyst for thermonuclear war began to seem like less of an accomplishment.

Sometimes I wondered why I had had to become psychotic before anybody recognized my illness for what it was, why nobody intervened before Gail. Anybody — that resident in my doctor's office, or a family member, or a library patron. Why was my editor the only person to note, "You're going nuts?"

I knew the reason: my crazy self looked too much like my regular self for people to see a change.

The doctors wouldn't give me a definite explanation as to why it had happened. But for me, the answer was clear. It was stress. A lack of sleep. It was triggered by an anti-malarial drug. It was genetic. It was me living out the act my mother had attempted when I was a child. It was society. It was this city, with its religious ways and welcome signs to Revelation. It was years of overcast skies. A crisis of the spirit. Bad karma. Bad decisions. Self-sabotage. Fear of success. It was symptomatic of a subtle shift in the fabric of life, caused by the internet. I had spent too much time in retail settings and they had debased me, undermined my humanity. It was just me. All me. A character flaw. Nerves. It was the fault of writing and reading, vulnerabilities they can make in a person. I could take all of those things, paste them onto a sheet of paper, look at them until they became glue-rippled and sun-faded, and still feel dissatisfied. Some seemed plausible, others less so, and then something like "flea markets" or "leprechauns" would appear in the mix and look plainly wrong. It was the whole thing.

Nothing good came out of my time in the ward. It was awful. I don't like the tendency to review a bad period and try to swing it around so hard that something positive is flung out. I disapprove.

But also, can't resist.

At the beginning of my first stay in the ward, for example, I had repeatedly been surprised to see Michelle return. This belonged to my paranoid mindset: of course she came back. Visiting is what people do for a loved one in hospital, especially a spouse. That I placed so much importance on her returns was another sign of my delusions. On the other hand, the viewpoint was valuable, even if temporary and from a delusional state. I remember seeing her arrive and feeling the relief, the immeasurable relief: I can summon it now, palpably, and maybe that serves a purpose, a compression of all the small gratitudes one feels over a lifetime but seldom in so concentrated a form, a moment of pure thanks for a person that you can always return to, remember, feel.

I considered my reasons for writing about India, a place I hadn't been but somehow preferred over the city where I actually found myself. Slowly I understood that hating where you come from was only a few steps away from hating yourself, and I needed to change that, to adjust my feelings, swing them around, if only to avoid another breakdown. I had to remember an evening after my discharge, when Michelle needed to go somewhere but didn't like to leave me alone, and her father Dave dragged me over to his house to watch a video (*Dead Man Walking*). And that her mother, when I was heavily drugged and vacant of motivation, smuggled me away to help me get Christmas shopping done, having realized I would not accomplish this on my own. Without forgiving the place its flaws, I should remember that through it all, people were there for me, there.

And self-awareness is useful. When I saw my novel's publication approaching, I had the uneasy feeling that this futuristic, fanciful tale set in a distant place nevertheless contained all there was to know about me. But maybe, I eventually had to admit, the descent that accompanied it more truly reflected me. That was the story. It had been coming for a while. And now I knew it, and could refer to it in the future. I would remember it whenever I called a "hallway" a "whorehouse" or wished someone a "good dinosaur."

In my office, I reshuffled the books on my shelves. I had done so periodically in the past, purges to get rid of books that weren't me any more. *Silence of the Lambs*? I didn't like psychiatric problems as plot contrivances any more. *The Stand?* No, not me any more. *Misery?* Gone. What about *The Waves*? How about *The Waves*?

And of course, *The Loggers*. That one would have to stay; in fact it begged for a new category, on a more prominent shelf. The truth was I didn't like to blame reading or writing for what happened. When asking myself what made for my unbalanced mind, I preferred to push aside ideas of fault and think of my books as, at worst, symptoms of instability, and even then, mostly happy ones.

ACKNOWLEDGEMENTS

MICHELLE SUPPORTED ME BEFORE, during and after the period described in this book, and I don't know if I could have survived it without her. I thank her, and I thank all of the physicians, psychiatrists and hospital staff members who helped me. For their great personal support I would also like to express my gratitude to the Henn family, Gail and Klaus Berger, Erik Jensen, Mary and Dave Casey, James and Debbie Southwell, Robin Fairbridge, Gorm and Bolette Hansen, Kathy Brown and Art Anderson. Thanks also to Adam Lewis Schroeder and my wife for reading an early draft of the book and providing insightful feedback.

I am very fortunate to be able to say Derek Fairbridge is my friend, and remained one through the editing of this book and the events described within. For helping to make this book happen at Raincoast, I would also like to thank Michelle Benjamin, Jesse Finkelstein and Dan Werb.

The excerpt from Oliver Morton's review, "Dust Devils," appears courtesy of the author and the magazine that first published it, *The New Yorker*.

Time-Life Books published *The Loggers* in 1976 with text by Richard L. Williams.